QUIVEY'S GROVE
Heritage Cookbook

QUIVEY'S GROVE
Heritage Cookbook

Margaret Guthrie

Illustrations by Nancy Lynch

QUIVEY'S GROVE
PRAIRIE OAK PRESS
Madison, Wisconsin

First edition, first printing

Published by Prairie Oak Press for Quivey's Grove Restaurant

Copyright © 1994 by Margaret E. Guthrie

Prairie Oak Press

821 Prospect Place

Madison, Wisconsin 53703

Designed by Jane Tenenbaum, Tenenbaum Design, Madison, Wisconsin

Printed in the United States of America by BookCrafters, Chelsea, Michigan

Library of Congress Cataloging-in-Publication Data

Guthrie, Margaret E.

Quivey's Grove heritage cookbook / Margaret Guthrie

       c. cm.

   ISBN 1-879483-18-1 : $14.95

   1. Quivey's Grove (Restaurant : Madison, Wis.) 2. Cookery, American—Midwestern style.

   I. Title.

TX715.2.M53G88   1994

641.5'09775'83—dc20   94-9407

                                          CIP

CONTENTS

ACKNOWLEDGMENTS

A cookbook, particularly one based on recipes from a restaurant, is the work of many people. Without Joe Garton, who first saw the stone farmhouse and stable and knew immediately that it could make a splendid restaurant, there would have been no Quivey's Grove, therefore no book. I must also thank Craig Kuenning, who worked closely with me to be sure the recipes selected truly reflected Quivey's Grove food, atmosphere and history. I would also like to thank Jack Holzhueter for sharing his encyclopedic knowledge of local history. Perhaps the people who should be thanked most are the ones who participated in cutting down and testing the recipes. Five students in the baking class in the culinary trades department at Madison Area Technical College (MATC) cut down and tested all the muffin recipes. They are Tom Padron, Jeanette Schuetz, Mike Gosdeck, Richard Wiseman, and Matt Michaud. Also at MATC, Paul Short's Gourmet Dining class cut down and tested two recipes for this book. Then there is my loyal and hardworking core of recipe testers: Terese Allen, Ann Behrmann and her son, Lars Koch, Pamela Lundgren, Alice Pauser, Amy Schulz, and Carl Swanson. Thank you all.

Margaret E. Guthrie

I am most indebted to two people. Both have worked with me at Quivey's since before our opening, but are much more than great employees. With a constant turnover, probably more than five hundred employees in fifteen years, being able to rely on a few constants is essential. Craig Kuenning and Paul Hellenbrand are the constants at Quivey's Grove. Paul's enthusiasm, patience, and effort are inspiring. Craig has, at one time or another, done everything at Quivey's and, in doing it so well, made Quivey's Grove his own. He has my respect, affection, and gratitude.

Joe Garton

For me, this book chronicles a journey of almost fifteen years, starting with the renovation of Quivey's Grove, when I was a better carpenter than cook. The journey took me from pounding nails to pounding schnitzels to the present, where I seem to be pounding a computer keyboard rather than actually doing any cooking. Along the way there have been many people who have contributed recipes, ideas, foodstuffs, time and energy to collectively create the food at Quivey's Grove. We have used recipes from Joe Garton's family and many from my own family, adapting each to recreate the memories of family dining as we grew up. Customers have given us their own family recipes, as dining with us stirred memories. We have developed a network of people who bring us fresh raspberries and strawberries from their gardens, morel mushrooms from the forests and abandoned orchards, fresh asparagus from their backyards, apples from their orchards, tomatoes, rhubarb, and zucchini from their gardens, watercress from the spring on their land, and pumpkins, gourds, and Indian corn to decorate the restaurant in the fall. We have formed partnerships with our suppliers, most of whom have done business with us from the start, to provide us with the finest of meats and poultry from the Midwest, fresh fish, some locally raised, others from Midwest fisheries. We have a bounty of foodstuffs in the Midwest and we try to use it all.

Then there are the people who take this food, these recipes and ideas, and make them work. All of the people who have worked in the kitchen and the dining rooms, bar, and office here at Quivey's can take pride in knowing they had their hand in making this book happen. Long ago I realized it was not what I could do, personally, but what everyone around me could do. I don't think many people realize what all the people who work in a restaurant really do to make that meal special, but it is obvious to me that Quivey's Grove has some special people.

Craig Kuenning

AN INTRODUCTION TO QUIVEY'S GROVE

What is Quivey's Grove? There is a sentence on the menu that says it best: "Other restaurants are *in* Wisconsin, Quivey's Grove *is* Wisconsin!" How did this one-of-a-kind restaurant come about? The story begins a century and a half ago.

In 1855 in the village of Fitchburg, just outside of Madison, John Mann built a large house with a stable for his livery business just to the rear, both easily visible from the road. At the time, Fitchburg had a most successful inn, its first, which was called Quivey's Grove. More than 120 years later, this inn served as the inspiration for naming the restaurant.

Mann had come to Madison from New York via Michigan. By 1850 he had established a successful livery stable in town. In 1855 he moved to Fitchburg, where he built his mansion and a new livery stable, just off the road. He built the house of stone from a nearby quarry, for which he traded lumber from his land. The house also was built with cement cornices, a feature unique to the Italianate style then popular. The name of the builder or architect is unknown.

The road going past Mann's home and business led to Madison in one direction and to Mineral Point and southwestern Wisconsin in the other, making it a route of major importance. The agricultural economy of the area was expanding rapidly, and there were flourishing lead mines in the Mineral Point region. Mann's livery rented horses, carriages, and wagons, and offered stabling for horses. Blacksmith services might have been available as well. It was an ideal time to be in the livery business.

According to Jack Holzhueter of the State Historical Society of Wisconsin, the Mann farm was "the 1850s version of the corporate farm. It was large in terms of acreage and Mann probably employed many workers to farm the land he owned. He probably also kept his house in town from which he conducted his business affairs and where he would have been joined by his wife and children on occasion."

Also, according to Holzhueter, the land would be sold off in parcels to immigrants of modest means, who would build homesteads and begin farming on their own. Scattered over southern Wisconsin are many remnants of these large farms, of which Quivey's Grove is one of the best-known examples.

In 1855 when Mann built his place, Madison was still a town, not to be incorporated as a city until the following year. It was chosen as the territorial capital back in 1836, when it was nothing more than an isthmus of wild, overgrown land owned by James Duane Doty, who, with a handful of fellow speculators, had purchased the land between the lakes and then promoted it skillfully to the legislature which was responsible for choosing the location of the state capital. (More than a few of the legislators allegedly bought lots from Doty at prices as low as ten cents each, shortly before or shortly after casting their ballots.) There were twenty candidates for the honor, but Doty, according to David Mollenhoff's book *Madison: A History of the Formative Years*, was able to present "a well-located, thoughtfully designed product over which he could exercise complete control, a thorough understanding of territorial politics, and the friendship of several delegates [to the state legislature], an unrivaled knowledge of the territory, a superb grasp of human nature and a network of influential friends in Washington, D.C."

Remember that at this time the Wisconsin territory included all of Iowa and Minnesota and the eastern portion of both Dakotas. Half the population of the territory lived west of the Mississippi river. Delegates from this western area were aware that more than one state would be carved out of this territory. To them, a Wisconsin capital that would create no rivalry when the time came for a capital to be established in their western regions was most desirable. Madison seemed ideal for that reason.

Additionally, Doty had visited all of the other nineteen proposed sites while the majority of the delegates had seen at most two or three of the proposed capitals. Doty was in a position to be knowledgeably persuasive.

Once Madison was chosen, Doty moved to consolidate the town's position as permanent capital of the fledgling state by selling lots to the most prominent people he could, including eastern speculators like John Jacob Astor, who bought two dozen lots.

With news of the selection, the first people to move to the new site were Eben and Rosaline Peck, who packed up their belongings and moved from Blue Mounds to the "wilderness" at Madison. There, they purchased two lots for a hundred dollars each and erected a four-room cabin which they opened as a tavern and inn. Thus began Madison in 1837.

Eleven years later, Wisconsin was declared a state and Madison was made the permanent capital and home of the University of Wisconsin. During the next eight years the town grew from a wide spot in the road to an economic boom town.

In 1854, one year before Mann built his home, Horace Greeley, editor of the *New York Tribune*, paid a visit and wrote this account in his newspaper: "Madison has the most magnificent site of any inland town I ever saw.... The University crowns a beautiful eminence a mile west of the Capitol with a main street connecting them a la Pennsylvania Avenue. There are more comfortable private mansions now in progress in Madison than in any other place I have visited... Madison has a glorious career before her."

The same year that Greeley visited, the railroad arrived in Madison. In the nineteenth century, any town's success was dependent on railroad access—and now Madison had that, too.

Despite the feverish pace of building and expansion, Madisonians had ample leisure time for sports and games. One of the most popular was horse racing. In the beginning, races were held on a one-mile stretch of Williamson street between Blount Street and the Yahara river. A livery business certainly would have flourished in such an atmosphere, which is probably why John Mann prospered sufficiently to build his grand stone mansion in Fitchburg.

By 1855, those owning the "fast stock" had organized themselves into the Wisconsin Sporting Association. The association offered significant prize money, which attracted high-quality racing horses to the town. Winter races were held on the ice on Lake Monona, and eventually spring and summer races were held on a graded oval track where Orchard Ridge is today.

Madison's population doubled between 1849 and 1851, and doubled again between 1851 and 1853. John Mann had picked the perfect time and place to build his livery business. A resident of Madison reported that immigrants were "pouring in like a deluge" and that the streets were filled with covered wagons and herds of cattle. Many were on their way to Minnesota, Iowa, and northwestern Wisconsin, but many others stayed to settle. John Mann prospered, serving both new arrivals and older residents

In 1876 Mann sold his Fitchburg property to a J. C. Latham. In 1881 Latham sold out to J. R. Comstock, who owned the property until 1935. It was then purchased by Hal Huddleston, who sold it in 1948 to William Waskow. The Waskow family lived on the property, raising dogs in a kennel and horses in the stable, until 1979. In the spring of that year a mare gave birth to a foal, and the Waskows' horses then exceeded the horse population allowed by the local zoning laws. They decided to keep the horses and put up the property for sale.

At the time, Joe Garton was looking for a new family home. In touring the Waskow farm, he recognized immediately that the property did not have enough land for his needs, but he admired the stone house and barn. And, considering the closeness of the buildings to Verona Road, and the density of population within easy driving distance, it occurred to him that this would be a good spot for a restaurant.

"I had no thought of going into the restaurant business at that time," he says now, smiling slightly at the recollection. He was teaching film at the University of Wisconsin-Extension, and was thinking about opening a movie theater that served good food. But something about the Waskow place stirred his imagination, and before long he had committed himself to becoming a restaurateur.

The restaurant conversion took the better part of a year—six months in the planning and six more in construction. Not only was there a great deal of work required, but Joe was determined to preserve the historical and architectural integrity of both buildings. (Both are now on the National Register of Historical Places.)

The house, an Italianate fieldstone mansion with eighteen-inch thick walls and thirteen-foot ceilings, was in relatively good shape. The newel post and banisters on the front staircase are the original black walnut. Joe tore up the ancient linoleum, finding to his delight that it had long protected beautiful original hemlock flooring. The flooring is enjoyed by everyone today, although it must be refinished each year with four coats of polyurethane to protect against all those feet coming and going.

Bathrooms and a new entryway were added, using worm-eaten elm paneling rescued from other nineteenth-century farm buildings that were being torn down. A kitchen was added to the back of the house, along with a smaller service kitchen directly above it, and a dumbwaiter to connect them. A walk-in cooler was added at the same time. Joe gives credit for the design to architect Arlan Kay, whose firm specializes in historic restoration and remodeling.

The stable posed more serious problems. Horses had been living in the structure for 130 years. Most of the original structure could be preserved (the original stone walls are twenty inches thick), but the wooden floor had to be completely replaced. The walls were pressure-washed, but no technology exists to get more than a century of horse manure out of porous wood flooring. A new floor was laid and "aged" by beating it with bicycle chains, stained several times, and sealed with four coats of polyurethane. Two staircases were added, leading up to the "haymow." Old-time notching techniques were employed in its construction. The stable was furnished with rough-hewn chairs and tables, some made from old wagon wheels by two Wisconsin woodworkers. A hanging lantern is the work of a Wisconsin blacksmith.

During the planning stage, Garton anticipated a problem with the stone house dining rooms being thirty yards distant from the stable tap, where patrons would have a cocktail while waiting for their table to be ready. In the frigid depths of winter, the separate buildings would require patrons to bundle up and walk across the driveway. The first solution proposed was a covered walkway. Joe turned that down because the drawings "looked like a 1950s motel." The next idea struck home—to construct a tunnel that would connect the stable and the house, thus offering protection to patrons without disturbing the outdoor landscape. A tunnel, which also incorporates a wine cellar, was built using nearly fifty tons of stone. The gates guarding the wine rack are the work of the same Wisconsin blacksmith who fashioned the hanging lantern in the Stable Tap.

Jim Kuenning was the construction manager for the tunnel project. He saw that the new restaurant had real potential and so suggested to his son, Craig, who was then working in a Madison restaurant, that he get in on the ground floor of this new operation. As it happened, Craig got in *under* the ground floor, beginning by working on the tunnel construction. After the restaurant opened, Craig started working in the kitchen and learning the chef's trade. He has been with Quivey's Grove ever since, graduating from prep cook to line cook to his present position of executive chef and manager.

The tunnel was an instant hit. Many people today, looking at the rough stonework, assume that the tunnel was a part of the original farm, and some even believe it was part of the fabled "underground railroad" that escorted escaped slaves from the South to freedom in Canada. They are surprised when told that the tunnel was built in 1980.

While the restaurant construction was going on, Joe began to shop for suitable furnishings. On one trip to Chicago he found the penny dreadfuls that are now framed and hanging in the Valentine Room. Called penny dreadfuls because they cost a penny and delivered a humorously dreadful message, they were sent at a time when recipients of letters paid the postage.

Essentially, the recipient paid to be insulted. Two of the best:

Wanted

You bought the license and the ring
And then his praises began to sing,
But when he saw you, lightly drest,
He gladly took the first train West.

and

No Amount of Money Would Make You Acceptable

Were you in money up to the ear,
As by the artist pictured here,
You're such a rank and hopeless goose
That for you I'd still have no use.

The Valentine Room features hand-stencils by Jan Smart and Carolyn Malm. The room has been the site of countless marriage proposals, many made on Valentine's Day itself.

Joe discovered a treasure trove of Wisconsin sheet music in his grandparents' attic. He added to that collection and had the best pieces framed and hung, some in the Music Room and the rest in the Stable Tap. In the nineteenth century, home entertainment often centered around the piano, and piano sheet music was as popular then as video tapes are today. There were hundreds of sheet music publishers, not only in New York but all across the country, many of the songs written locally and many of those extolling the virtues and beauty of the locale in which they were sold. The walls of the Music Room are lined with such sheet music, thus preserving such timeless classics as, "I'm Going Back to Wisconsin Where the Money Grows on Trees."

The farmers in Wisconsin sure must live a life of ease
Why they just work up an appetite and rest under the trees
I have lived in New York City and I know just how it feels
When you have to keep on rushing or they'll step right on your heels

I'm going to Wisconsin and I'm going to stay right there
It sort of peps you up when you breathe Wisconsin air
So I'm going to Wisconsin where I'll live a life of ease
To the land of milk and honey where the money grows on trees

In the early 1930s, the following brought a tear to many an eye:

Take Me Back to Dear Wisconsin

They sing of old Kentucky
The Swanee river too

The beautiful Ohio
The Carolina moon
We know that old Virginia
Is surely mighty fine
But give me old Wisconsin
In the good old summertime

(chorus)

Take me back to dear Wisconsin
God's great northern clime
In that land of gorgeous beauty
Ev'rything is fine
The angels smiled upon it
And made it so sublime
Just give me old Wisconsin
In the good old summertime

And here are just a couple of lines from a song that saluted one of our favorite towns (and Joe Garton's home town), "She-Boy-Gan":

It's a nice little city where the girls are pretty
The boys you'll find are the regular kind

Next door, in the nursery, are framed illustrations from a charming book of nursery rhymes. Guests are asked to see how many familiar rhymes they can name, based on the illustrations. It was in this room that an older woman guest once told her waitress, "You don't need to tell me anything about this house, I was born in this room."

On the stairs and in the hallway of the house is a veritable political history of the state and nation. There is a lithograph of Wisconsin governors from 1844 to 1878, a Harding and Coolidge campaign poster, and an engraving of Congressman Garfield that predates 1880 when on the 36th ballot he became the GOP presidential nominee. Framed and hanging over the stairs is a rare original campaign poster for the Republican Party candidates Fremont and Shearman from the election of 1856, the year after Quivey's was built. (John C. Fremont was the first presidential nominee of the newly formed Republican Party, and was defeated by James Buchanan.) Downstairs is a fascinating group portrait of the first 25 presidents of the United States, presumably not executed during a single sitting of the subjects. Flanking the stairs is a collection of antique lithographs and engravings of Madison sites, including the original state capitol, the University of Wisconsin campus, the fish hatchery, and an ice boating scene on Lake Mendota.

In the "Flower Box" room, on the first floor, is an antique walnut cupboard with an elaborate apron and an ogee-curved cornice typical of cupboards made between 1820 and 1860. Between the windows in this room is a hand-colored lithograph from 1846, "Tree of Liberty," honoring all the states of the union. (Observers will note that Wisconsin was not then a state.) Also in this room are eight hand-colored botanical prints, antique china, a U.S. map, and a political cartoon, all from the nineteenth century.

There is a quilt hanging in each of the downstairs dining rooms, and each room is named for the pattern of its quilt. In the central hall, an old church lectern is used as a reservation desk. A built-in cupboard houses a collection of old china, most of which has been donated by patrons of the restaurant. Joe has been amazed at the number of people who bring family treasures to Quivey's, suggesting that they be displayed in the house for others to enjoy. Quivey's has a way of touching people's memory and appreciation of the past, and of encouraging them to share it with others.

By 1988 the size of the stable was inadequate. The informal, relaxed atmosphere and hearty food attracted a large and loyal following that just kept growing. An addition was made in 1989 using worm-eaten wood and old beams salvaged from nearby barns that had been torn down. So carefully was the project designed and carried out that today it is difficult to tell where the old stable ends and the addition begins.

The stable is decorated with fascinating odds and ends. There is a framed cover of a 1948 edition of *Life* magazine naming Madison the ideal American city in which to live. There is a mounted buffalo head on permanent loan from a former employee and a reproduction of an 1855 American flag. Over the bar hang two beer trays depicting William Jennings Bryan and William McKinley in the presidential race of 1896. Perhaps the most interesting item in the stable is a photograph by Joe Garton of the interior of the structure, when it really was a stable, that reminds him of the first time he walked through it, knee-deep in hay, the aroma of horse manure hanging heavy in the air.

From that moment of inspiration until the present, Quivey's Grove has grown through the imagination, planning, and creation of many devoted people. It is a graceful merging of old and new, offering a unique gathering place for friends and family. Quivey's Grove is a warm place in which to discover some of Wisconsin's most fascinating roots—and perhaps to remind you of some of your own.

The Recipes

Nancy Lynch

Special Occasions

Quivey's Grove puts its whole heart into special occasions. Holidays are celebrated here as they are in private homes. Guests are cheered by the special preparations and the atmosphere of good will and anticipation. Visitors at Christmastime are greeted with gaily decorated trees, garlands of balsam, cheerful wreaths, and sparkling candlelight. Valentine's Day welcomes lovers, old and young, with big red hearts and a very special menu. Easter, Mother's Day, Father's Day, Thanksgiving—each receives its thoughtful due at Quivey's, in both decoration and menu preparation.

Personal special occasions are also honored. Many a bride and groom have chosen to have their wedding at Quivey's because of the sense of occasion and extra effort that goes into the staff's preparation for these celebrations. Many hold the actual wedding ceremony at Quivey's, often outdoors on the beautiful grounds. A Victorian wedding breakfast? An evening wedding luau? The bride and groom departing in a horse-drawn carriage? Quivey's is pleased to accommodate. One bride and groom even departed dramatically in a hot-air balloon—arranged by the Quivey's staff.

Quivey's is the place to honor Mother on her birthday, fete a colleague on retirement, entertain an important out-of-town visitor, wish a bon voyage to a special friend. The staff's special attention to detail, and sensitivity to the needs of the occasion, set Quivey's Grove apart from other restaurants.

Through the years, special menus and recipes have been developed to honor all these holidays and special occasions. Here are some you might wish to incorporate into your own celebrations.

DINNER FOR A SPECIAL OCCASION

Country pâtés

Duck and cherry tarts

Smoked trout and roasted red pepper terrine

Roasted chicken breast with apple, dried cherry, and black walnut stuffing

Sweet potato shoestrings

Cranberry chutney

Chocolate truffles

Black walnut tart with maple cream

Coffee

Sautéed apples often accompany entrées at Quivey's. Delicious at any time of year, they are especially appropriate during the early fall apple harvest when many varieties are available and fresh.

Quivey's Sautéed Apples

4 apples, peeled, cored, cut in 1-inch chunks
2 teaspoons butter
$^1/_2$ cup sugar

. . . . .

Melt the butter in large sauté pan. Add the apples, sprinkle them with the sugar, and sauté. Stir the apples to coat them with the butter as they cook. Cook just until the apples are soft but not mushy. Serve hot. Yield: 4 servings.

Three commercial apple varieties trace their roots to the Wisconsin landscape. The Wolf River apple was first discovered on a farm outside Fremont, in Waupaca County. A large apple, it can weigh as much as two pounds and is used primarily for cooking. The Northwestern Greening, another good cooking apple from the same area of the state, and the McMahon White, which originated around Richland Center, are the other two.

Applesauce is another popular fall dish at the restaurant. You can make a big batch when the harvest comes in, then freeze it in jars for use throughout the year.

Applesauce

24 apples
Water, lemon juice
2 cups sugar
1 teaspoon allspice

. . . . . .

Peel, core, and cut apples into ³/₄-inch chunks. Keep the prepared apples in the water and lemon juice to prevent discoloring until all the apples are ready for cooking.

Place the apples in a heavy-bottom saucepan over medium heat. Cook until the apples are very soft, but not mushy. Remove from heat. Add the sugar and allspice. Stir well, mash slightly and serve warm. Remaining applesauce should be chilled. Yield: 12 servings.

Wisconsin produced 54 million pounds of apples in 1992, ranking the state eighteenth among the nation's producers. About one-fifth of the Wisconsin crop is used in processed products—primarily cider, applesauce, and pie filling.

Cranberries are a native American fruit that quickly became highly prized by European immigrants. The American Heritage Cookbook says, "Cranberries may have been known at first as 'crane berries,' since cranes living in the New England bogs ate the berries. They were recognized early as a good preventive of scurvy. Ships putting out to sea from Down East ports always carried casks of this 'bog medicine' in their stores." In the 1600s they were also known as bounce berries for their ability to bounce. Indeed, their ability to bounce is still a test for ripeness in cranberries.

Cranberry Chutney

1 tablespoon olive oil
1 tablespoon chopped fresh sage
$^3/_4$ cup brown sugar
2-3 apples, cored and diced
$^1/_2$ cup chopped hazelnuts
$^1/_2$ cup cider vinegar
$^1/_2$ cup dry white wine
$^1/_2$ teaspoon minced red bell pepper
2 cups fresh whole cranberries
Salt to taste

Heat the oil in a heavy-bottom sauté pan. Add the sage and stir gently until it wilts and becomes aromatic. Add the sugar and stir to combine with the oil and sage. Wash the apples before chopping, but do not peel them. Add the apples, nuts, vinegar, wine, and cranberries, and simmer until thick. Add the red pepper as the mixture cooks. Once the mixture has reached the desired thickness, taste and add salt, if necessary. The tangy taste of cranberry chutney is a perfect complement to pork and turkey dishes. Yield: 1 pint.

Wisconsin is a major producer of cranberries, ranking right behind Massachusetts. The first recorded local trade in the beautiful red berries occurred in 1829 when a load was taken from Green Bay to market in Galena. Wisconsin devotes approximately 7,000 acres to cranberries, about the same acreage given to raising horseradish.

These elegant, bite-size potatoes are served at many Quivey's Grove weddings. They are an excellent finger food since the potato is firm and the whole thing can be popped into the mouth neatly. They are delicious, too.

Stuffed New Potatoes

12 walnut-size red new potatoes, unpeeled
Assorted cream cheese spreads (See Appetizers chapter)
Chives, parsley, crumbled cooked bacon, capers, chopped
    toasted nuts, etc. for garnish

. . . . .

Boil the potatoes until they can be pierced with a fork with just a little resistance. Drain and run them under cool water to stop the cooking. Cut a thin slice from each end and then cut each potato in half. With a melon baller, scoop out a cavity in each half potato.

When all the potatoes are prepared, fill a pastry bag fitted with a star tip with one of the cream cheese spreads and pipe into each potato. Use two or three different fillings. Garnish and place on a tray. Yield: 24 hors d'oeuvres.

Dried cherry fritters have been a feature of many Easter brunches at Quivey's. They are equally good just about any time of year—a great midwinter dessert, terrific with coffee in the early morning, welcome after a brisk cross-country ski.

Dried Cherry Fritters

1¹/₄ cups flour
1 tablespoon baking soda
2 tablespoons sugar
¹/₂ teaspoon salt
¹/₂ teaspoon allspice

2 eggs
1 cup buttermilk
1 tablespoon melted butter
1 cup dried sour cherries
Cinnamon sugar

. . . . . .

Mix dry ingredients. Beat eggs and buttermilk together in medium bowl. Add dried cherries to liquid. Add melted butter to liquid. Add dry ingredients to liquid all at once. Stir just to moisten. Heat canola or other light cooking oil to 350 degrees in a heavy, steep-sided saucepan. Drop by tablespoon carefully into hot oil. Cook for 5 minutes, letting the fritters turn themselves. Remove and drain on paper towels. While hot, dust with cinnamon sugar. Yield: 18 fritters.

Dried cherries are a Wisconsin product. Sour cherries are grown extensively in Door County, where the mitigating effects of Lake Michigan and Green Bay create a hospitable climate for cherry production.

Brunch is currently served at Quivey's only on Mother's Day, Father's Day, and Easter. On these special occasions, one of the dishes much favored is Wild Rice Pancakes. These are especially good served with locally made bacon or sausage, and with tangy sautéed apples (page 4).

Wild Rice Pancakes

₁/₂ cup flour
¹/₂ teaspoon baking soda
¹/₂ cup cornmeal
Salt & pepper to taste
1¹/₂ cups buttermilk
3 egg yolks
4 tablespoons melted butter
3 tablespoons maple syrup
1³/₄ cups cooked wild rice
¹/₂ cup toasted, chopped nuts
3 egg whites, beaten

. . . . . .

Combine the flour, baking soda, and cornmeal with salt and pepper to your taste. Beat together the buttermilk, egg yolks, butter, and maple syrup. Beat the egg whites until they hold stiff peaks.

Mix the flour and cornmeal with the buttermilk mixture, beating to blend thoroughly. Add in the wild rice and chopped nuts and mix well. Begin to heat the griddle for the pancakes. Fold in the beaten egg whites carefully. Grill the pancakes, cooking until all the batter is used up.

Yield: 24-36 (4-5 inch) pancakes.

A QUIVEY'S
SPRING
BRUNCH

(for Mother's Day or Easter)

Individual smoked gouda and onion quiches with ham crust

American fried potatoes

Fresh asparagus

Butter horns

Cinnamon rolls

Strawberry mini muffins

Dried cherry fritters

Lemon poppyseed bread

Smoked trout salad

Garlic toasts

Lemon curd tarts with strawberries

When chef Craig and his wife Bonnie held their wedding dinner at Quivey's, Craig came up with this recipe to celebrate the very special event:

Sterling Beef
with Gorgonzola Cream Sauce

Sterling Beef honors professor John Sterling, the sole U.W. faculty in 1849, who also ran a second-hand furniture store to supplement his yearly salary of $500.

6 (6-ounce) beef tenderloin filets
$^1/_2$ cup dried morel mushrooms
$^1/_2$ cup warm water
8 ounces shiitake mushrooms
4 ounces white mushrooms
4 ounces butter
2 cloves garlic, peeled, minced
$^1/_4$ cup Madeira wine
$^1/_2$ cup heavy cream
2 ounces Gorgonzola cheese
1 cup fresh bread crumbs
Salt & pepper to taste

With a small, sharp knife, make a slit in the side of each filet. Then work the knife inside the meat to make a pocket. Set filets aside.

Soak the morels in water for $^1/_2$ hour. Strain, saving the water. Remove the stems from the shiitakes and reserve for another use. Dice all the mushrooms and sauté over high heat in the butter. Add the garlic and continue to sauté until almost dry. Add the morel mushroom juice and again sauté until almost dry. Add the wine and the cream and reduce until the sauce coats a spoon thickly. Remove from heat and add cheese, stirring to melt and blend. Bind with bread crumbs. Add salt and pepper to taste and chill.

Stuff the filets with the mushroom mixture, then grill over high heat, turning once. Serve with Gorgonzola Cream Sauce. Yield: 6 servings.

Gorgonzola Cream Sauce

8 ounces shiitake mushrooms
5 tablespoons butter
$^1/_2$ cup water
White part of leek, washed & diced
2 garlic cloves, peeled & minced
1 tablespoon flour
1 cup whipping cream
6 ounces Gorgonzola cheese
Madeira
Salt & pepper to taste

. . . . .

Remove the stems from the shiitakes and sauté the stems in the butter with the stems from stuffing recipe (see previous page). Cover with water and cook slowly for 10 minutes. Strain this mixture, reserving the liquid, discarding the stems. Dice the shiitakes and sauté with the leek and garlic in the remaining butter. Add flour, stir, and cook 2 minutes. Add the cream and the reserved mushroom liquid and cook until it coats a spoon evenly. Stir in cheese until it melts. Add Madeira and adjust the seasoning with salt and pepper. Serve with the stuffed steaks. Yield: Sauce for 6 servings.

* This sauce can be made for other dishes just as directed. You won't have the extra shiittake stems, but it should not make a difference in the overall flavor or texture of the sauce.

UNIVERSITY COMMENCE-MENT DINNER

Morel and salmon strudel

Spinach salad with marinated mushrooms and tarragon vinaigrette

Smoked roasted prime rib of beef with whiskey peppercorn sauce

Garlic green onion bread pudding

Dairyland potatoes (twice-baked with cheese)

Turtle pie

At Thanksgiving, Quivey's has the atmosphere of a large and festive family gathering. A buffet of appetizers is set out in the stable, with cheeses, tiny onion tarts, smoked trout puffs, nuts, and raw vegetables with various dips. Guests can enjoy these while sipping their drinks before dinner. Then they walk through the tunnel to the house for the traditional sit-down Thanksgiving dinner of fresh turkey, cranberry chutney, and a variety of winter vegetables.

A roast turkey is the centerpiece of any Thanksgiving celebration worthy of the name. And, for many, a turkey may take center stage at Christmas or New Year's, and sometimes at Easter.

Roast Turkey
with Black Forest Walnut Stuffing

STUFFING

1 medium onion, peeled & diced	2 apples, cored & diced
2-3 ribs celery, diced	$^1/_2$ cup raisins
4 ounces butter or margarine (1 stick)	$^3/_4$ cup chopped walnuts
5 slices stale Black Forest rye bread, cut into $^1/_2$-inch cubes	$^1/_2$ teaspoon cinnamon
	$^1/_2$ teaspoon ginger
	$^1/_2$ teaspoon ground sage
	$^1/_2$ teaspoon salt or to taste
	Cider

THE TURKEY

12-15 pound turkey	Bay leaf
$^1/_2$ lemon	Onion
Salt & pepper	Whole cloves
Giblets	Peppercorns

· · · · · ·

Melt the butter or margarine in a large sauté pan. Sauté the onion and celery in the butter until soft.

Put the other ingredients in a large bowl and toss lightly to mix. Pour the onion mixture over all and mix again to blend the onion-celery mixture into the other ingredients. If the stuffing seems dry, moisten with cider. This amount of stuffing should be sufficient for a 12- to 15-pound turkey. Remember not to pack the stuffing in tightly or the turkey will be dry.

A fresh turkey is best. Prepare the bird by removing the giblets, liver, heart, and neck, which the processor stores in the turkey's abdominal cavity or breast cavity. Put these in a small, heavy-bottom saucepan with enough water to cover, add a bay leaf or two, an onion studded with cloves, and several peppercorns. Simmer, covered, until the meats are tender. Reserve this stock for the gravy.

Preheat oven to 350 degrees. Wash out the inside of the turkey with hot water and pat dry with paper towels. Rub cavities with a cut lemon, then sprinkle lightly with salt and a little freshly cracked pepper. Put the turkey in a large roasting pan, fold the wingtips under the first joint of each wing, and then put the stuffing in both cavities. Tie the legs together with butcher twine. Rub the skin with softened butter, sprinkle with thyme, and cover with the top of the roasting pan, or with an aluminum foil tent, making sure the foil does not touch the turkey's skin. Place the bird in the oven.

Allow twenty minutes to the pound. A 12-pound turkey will take 4 hours, approximately. During roasting, baste the turkey frequently so that the skin becomes golden brown and crispy. Uncover the last half hour or so. If the turkey skin starts to get too dark, cover it with a clean dishcloth that has been dampened and wrung out. When the turkey is done (juices run clear when the skin is pierced), remove it from the oven. Take it out of the roasting pan, put it on a heated platter, and cover it lightly with aluminum foil. Take drippings from the pan and put them into a large, heavy-bottom skillet. Sprinkle flour over the drippings and begin whisking over low to moderate heat to make a roux. As the roux thickens, begin to add some of the stock from the giblets. Use all the stock if necessary to make plenty of good, rich gravy. The giblets and liver should be chopped fine and added. Yield: 8-10 servings with plenty of leftovers.

Benjamin Franklin once wrote to his daughter that he regretted the choice of the bald eagle as our national bird for "he is a bird of bad moral Character, like those among men who live by sharping and robbing, he is generally poor and often lousy... The turkey is a much more respectable bird, and withal a true original Native of America."

For smaller families, a whole turkey may seem to be too much of a good thing. Here's a stuffed breast of turkey recipe that's perfect for a smaller family gathering or an elegant party.

Breast of Turkey
with Duck Sausage & Foie Gras Sauce

2 pounds duck breast meat
$^1/_2$ pound good-quality bacon
$^1/_2$ cup chopped parsley
3 teaspoons juniper berries
1 teaspoon nutmeg
2 teaspoons chopped garlic
4 shallots, chopped
2 eggs
$^1/_4$ cup whipping cream
3 tablespoons cognac
4-pound boneless turkey breast

. . . . . .

Dice the duck meat and bacon, put in the food processor and puree until the meat forms a smooth paste. Remove and put in a large bowl. Put the parsley, juniper berries, nutmeg, garlic, and shallots into the food processor and puree, then add to the duck mixture. Add the eggs, cream, and cognac to the mixture and mix well. Sauté a small piece, taste, and adjust seasonings. Set aside.

Preheat oven to 350 degrees. Remove the skin carefully, in one piece, from the turkey breast. With a sharp knife, carefully make several cuts in the breast to butterfly. The breast should open out enough to form a large rectangular piece of meat. Pound the turkey breast with a mallet till the meat is about $^1/_2$-inch thick.

Mrs. Stephen J. Field's Statesmen's Dishes and How to Cook Them, *published in 1890:*

"The turkey should be cooped up and fed some time before Christmas. Three days before it's slaughtered, it should have an English walnut forced down its throat three times a day and a glass of sherry once a day. The meat will then be deliciously tender, and have a fine nutty flavor."

And we think it's a problem to find a fresh turkey!

Spread the duck sausage stuffing over the entire turkey breast. Roll it up jellyroll fashion, and wrap it in the reserved turkey skin, tying it closed with butcher twine. Place in a roasting pan in $^1/_4$-inch water. Cover and roast for about $1^1/_2$ hours or until the meat at the center reaches 165 degrees on a meat thermometer.

Foie Gras Sauce

4 cups veal stock
8 cups turkey or chicken stock
4 tablespoons butter
4 tablespoons flour
$^1/_2$ pound fresh foie gras
1 tablespoon minced fresh sage
$^1/_2$ cup Gewurztztraminer wine

. . . . . .

Over medium heat, reduce the veal and turkey stock to 6 cups total. Add all the pan drippings from the roasted turkey to the stock and bring to a boil. Thicken with the roux made from the flour and butter, and cook on low heat for 10 minutes to reduce slightly. Add the wine.

Remove the turkey from the oven and allow it to sit for about 15 minutes. Remove string and skin from the breast and slice the roll into $^1/_4$-inch slices. Fan out two or three slices to a plate. Quickly sauté the foie gras, put a small piece on top of the turkey on each place, and pour some of the sauce over. Serve. Yield: 6 servings.

Christmas

Christmas is a special time at Quivey's Grove. All of the half-barrels that hold flowers in summer are filled with small evergreens, each strung with tiny white lights. The old apple tree in front of the stable, which blesses us with its fruit in the fall, also sparkles with lights.

Indoors, fresh live greens are placed everywhere there is place to hang them or a niche to hold them. A 24-foot balsam evergreen tree dominates the stable, its topmost branches reaching up the stairwell into the second floor. Starting in November, members of the waitstaff spend spare moments in stringing popcorn and cranberries. One year, the chef made small people out of salt dough and painted each one to look like a member of the staff. Now, years later, newer staff members try to identify the "old-timers" represented by the salt-dough figures.

Early in the season, a decorating party is held that includes owners, staff, personal friends, loyal customers, and everybody's children. The kids are put to work making gingerbread houses and tree ornaments.

Food, of course, occupies the center of attention in the whirlwind of preparation. A special Christmas menu is printed up with entrees named for characters in Tchaikovsky's "Nutcracker Suite," Dickens' A Christmas Carol, *and several of Anthony Trollope's Christmas stories, all nineteenth-century favorites.*

For many immigrants from Europe, it wouldn't be Christmas without a Christmas goose. Quivey's pays honor to that custom with their own Goose Drosselmeyer, so named to honor that rather sinister and intriguing gentleman who presented Clara with the nutcracker. Remember, that's the nutcracker that became a Prince!

Goose Drosselmeyer

1 (8-pound) goose	$^1/_4$-$^1/_3$ cup flour
3 pounds sauerkraut	Fat from goose
2 cups cranberries	

STOCK MADE FROM GIBLETS

Giblets	Peppercorns
Water	Salt & pepper to taste
Onion	Kitchen Bouquet, if needed
Bay leaves	

. . . . . .

Have your butcher cut the goose into 8 pieces.

Put the giblets and neck of the goose in a deep saucepan with bay leaves, an onion, and peppercorns. Cover with water, put a lid on the pan, and simmer until the giblets, liver, and heart are tender.

Geese have a lot of surface fat on their skin. With a vegetable brush, wash the pieces of goose under hot water, brushing the skin vigorously. Cut away as much of the body fat as you can and discard. Preheat oven to 425 degrees.

Put the pieces of goose in a roasting pan about 6 inches deep. Put the pan in the oven and cook the goose for 30 minutes at 425 degrees. Remove the goose from the oven and place the pieces on a platter. Turn the oven down to 350 degrees.

Drain off the fat and spread the sauerkraut in the bottom of the pan. Sprinkle the cranberries on top of the sauerkraut, distributing them evenly. Place the pieces of goose on the

"We wish you a merry Christmas

And a happy New Year;

A pocket full of money

And a cellar full of beer,

And a great fat pig

To last you all the year."

—Traditional carol of first footers & Quivey's holiday greetings

bed of sauerkraut and cranberries and put the pan back in the oven. Roast for another hour and a half, draining off fat as necessary. Put about $^1/_3$-$^1/_2$ cup of fat into a sauté pan on top of the stove, discarding the rest.

After an hour and a half, take the roasting pan out of the oven and spoon some of the sauerkraut over the goose, settling the pieces down into the kraut cranberry mixture. Cook for another thirty minutes.

While the goose is cooking the last 30 minutes, cut up the giblets, mincing them very fine. Remove the neck meat and mince that also. Turn the sauté pan containing the duck fat on medium low, sprinkle the flour over the fat and begin to whisk. Mixture should thicken and cook a few minutes to remove any floury taste. Begin to add the stock made from boiling the giblets, about $^1/_2$ cup at a time, whisking continually. When the gravy is the consistency you like, add salt and pepper to taste and hold.

Should the color not be quite dark enough to suit you, add a little Kitchen Bouquet. Kitchen Bouquet is simply caramelized vegetables sold in small bottles. Its sole purpose is to make gravy a more attractive color. It will impart a deep rich brown without changing the flavor in any way.

"Christmas is a-comin'
The geese are getting fat,
Please to put a penny
In the old man's hat.
If you haven't got a penny
A ha'penny will do,
If you haven't got a ha'penny
Then God bless you."
— Old English rhyme

Easter is another busy time at Quivey's, a holiday when ham takes center stage. Here is Craig's recipe for home-cooked ham, demanded at Easter but also appreciated at New Year's or at any time there's a craving for it.

Easter Ham

1 whole, bone-in ham
2 medium onions, sliced
2 cups white wine
$^1/_2$ cup coarse grain Dijon-
    style mustard
1 cup brown sugar

1 cup demi-glace*
1 cup white wine
$^1/_2$ cup gherkin pickles,
    diced
$^1/_4$ teaspoon ground cloves
4 tablespoons cold butter

. . . . .

Preheat oven to 300 degrees. Wash the ham and place in a covered roasting pan with the onions and 2 cups of wine. Put the ham in the oven and cook for 3 hours, until tender. Remove from oven. Remove the ham from the roaster and let it cool slightly. Skim the fat from the pan juices and add wine. Bring the pan juices to a boil and scrape up all the brown bits. Strain this into a saucepan. Reduce to 1 cup, add the demi-glace and bring to a boil. Add the diced pickles and the clove and hold warm.

Heat oven to 375 degrees. Remove the skin from the ham. Remove as much fat as you wish, but leave at least $^1/_4$ inch. Score the fat in a diamond pattern. Mix the mustard and brown sugar to a paste and coat the ham. Return the ham to the oven to glaze, about 20 minutes. Remove from the oven and let stand another 20 minutes. Just before carving, reheat the sauce, whisk in the cold butter. Slice the ham and serve the sauce over it. Yield: 8-10 servings with leftovers.

* Demi-glace is veal stock that has been reduced almost to a syrup. It is thick, dark brown, and loaded with flavor. It's now possible to purchase it in some gourmet shops.

Nancy Lynch

Appetizers &
Hors d'Oeuvres

The difference between an appetizer and an hors d'oeuvre is not widely appreciated. An appetizer is something served at the beginning of the meal, intended to beguile the appetite and set the stage for bigger and better things to come. An hors d'oeuvre is usually some bite-size delicacy that may serve as an appetizer, but may also stand alone as finger food served at a cocktail party or reception, with no formal meal to follow.

> "The cocktail party, with its rounds of drinks and trays of hors d'oeuvres, did not come into vogue until the twentieth century. Previously, guests were invited for dinner rather than just for drinks. Appetizers and canapes were rarely served, except, perhaps, for a half-dozen oysters before the soup."
>
> —*American Heritage Cookbook*

That half-dozen oysters may be what has led us to the present day when appetizers have become a popular way to introduce a dinner. Quivey's has both appetizers that bring on the meal and hors d'oeuvres that are served at wedding receptions, cocktail parties, and other events attended by many people who do not sit down to a formal meal.

Duck Nibblers

MARINADE
$^3/_4$ cup soy sauce
$^1/_4$ cup water
1 tablespoon Dijon-style mustard
2 cloves garlic, minced
1 teaspoon minced fresh ginger
2 teaspoons Chinese five spice powder
2 tablespoons honey

1 pound duck breast, skinless & boneless
2 eggs
4 tablespoons water
1 cup fine pretzel crumbs
$^1/_2$ cup barbecue sauce
$^1/_4$ cup raspberry jam

Mix marinade ingredients together, beating to blend well. Slice the duck breast into strips about $^1/_2$-inch thick and marinate for 1 hour. Drain. Heat the barbecue sauce and raspberry jam together on low heat. Beat eggs with water. Dip the duck strips first in the egg wash, then in the pretzel crumbs. Saute in hot oil for 3-4 minutes to medium rare on inside. Serve with barbecue sauce. Yield: 6-8 servings, if served with other finger foods.

These meatballs may be served with your favorite barbecue sauce, or a sour cream sauce with dill for a Swedish taste, or a sweet-and-sour sauce for an Oriental flavor.

Meatballs

1 pound ground beef
$^1/_2$ pound ground pork
$^1/_2$ cup finely diced onion
1 cup fresh bread crumbs
3 eggs
$^1/_2$ cup milk
$^1/_2$ teaspoon Tabasco sauce
Splash of Worcestershire sauce
$^1/_2$ teaspoon freshly ground black pepper

. . . . .

Preheat oven to 350 degrees. Lightly grease a cookie sheet. Mix all the ingredients together and shape into balls about the size of a walnut (in the shell). Place on the cookie sheet. Place the sheet in the oven and bake for 10-12 minutes. Remove and put the meatballs in chosen sauce. Yield: about 24 small meatballs.

*Onion Tartlets
honor James
Strang, who
founded a
Mormon
community on
Beaver Island in
1847 and declared
himself king and
the new prophet
of the Mormon
Church.*

This recipe is popular with guests at Quivey's for private cocktail parties. When these are made as tarts and appear on the menu as an appetizer, they are called King James Strang Onion Tarts.

Onion Tartlets

PASTRY
$2^1/_2$ cups flour
1 cup butter, cut in chunks
1 teaspoon salt
1 teaspoon Tabasco sauce
$^2/_3$ cup freshly grated Parmesan cheese
5 tablespoons cold water

FILLING
1 large onion, diced fine
1 leek (white part), cleaned and diced fine
1 bunch green onions, diced fine
1 teaspoon minced garlic
4 tablespoons butter
1 teaspoon salt
2 tablespoons flour
$^1/_2$ cup + 2 tablespoons whipping cream
2 ounces mild cheese
Freshly grated black pepper

· · · · ·

Place the flour, butter, salt, Tabasco, and cheese in the work bowl of a food processor. Process until grainy. Add water, a spoonful at a time, until the dough begins to adhere to the sides of the bowl. Stop and scrape the dough out onto a floured board. Flour a rolling pin and roll dough to about $^1/_4$- to $^1/_8$-inch thickness, as for pie crust.

Preheat oven to 325 degrees. Cut with small biscuit cutter and place each round on the back of a fluted tartlet pan. Put another on top of the pastry and invert the two. Put tartlets on a cookie sheet. Continue until all the pans are pastry lined. Bake about 5-8 minutes. Remove from oven and cool.

For the filling: Melt 2 tablespoons of butter in a heavy-bottom sauté pan and add the onion, leek, green onion, and garlic. Sprinkle with salt and add 2 tablespoons of cream, stirring to mix well. Cook, covered, over low to wilt.

In another pan, melt the remaining butter, stir in the flour. Cook for a few minutes over low heat, stirring constantly. Stir in the remaining cream until thickened, then remove from heat. Put the cheese in the food processor and process. Add the onion mixture and process until grainy. Add the bechamel (the flour-butter-cream mixture) and the pepper and mix well. Spoon into the tart shells, sprinkle tops with a little paprika for color, and bake for 5-8 minutes or until the filling sets up. Serve at once. Yield: 80 small tartlets.

For a cocktail party, figure on 8 hors d'oeuvres per individual. Some will eat less, some will eat more. It's to be hoped that no one will stuff their pockets or handbags with the nibbles, thereby skewing the numbers.

In spring, Quivey's buys as many morels as they are offered, often as many as 250 pounds, freezing what is not immediately used.

Salmon & Wild Mushroom Pastries

1 pound fresh salmon filets
8 ounces wild mushrooms (shiitake, morel, chanterelle or oyster)
8 ounces butter, room temperature
2 tablespoons chopped fresh chervil
2 tablespoons chopped fresh chives
1 tablespoon chopped fresh dill weed
2 tablespoons minced garlic
2 tablespoons white wine
4 ounces butter, melted
4 sheets phyllo dough
Salt & pepper to taste

· · · · · ·

Clean and dice the mushrooms, then saute them in 2 oz. of the butter. Skin and remove the bones of the salmon; cut meat into cubes. In a food processor, combine the remaining butter, herbs, garlic and wine. Blend until smooth. Combine the salmon and mushrooms with the butter mixture. Refrigerate for 10 minutes.

Preheat the oven to 350 degrees. Take 2 sheets of the phyllo dough and place one on top of the other. Cut in half lengthwise. Brush with the melted butter. Repeat with the other two sheets. Divide the salmon filling into 4 parts and place one part at the edge of each pastry strip. Fold up into a triangle the way you would fold up a flag. Repeat with each strip, place on baking sheet. Brush with butter.

Bake for 15 minutes or until golden brown. Serve at once. Yield: 4 appetizers.

There is a special Wisconsin mystique about morel mushrooms. Untold thousands of state residents comb the woods and fields every spring in search of this elusive fungus. A successful morel hunter would no more reveal a secret cache than would a trout angler share a special hidden stream. Morel etiquette demands that the hunter not pick all the morels in any given spot, leaving a few behind to produce spore for next year's crop.

Stuffed Mushrooms

12 - 18 large mushroom caps*
1¹/₂ pounds mushrooms, including stems from large
    mushrooms
2¹/₂ slices bacon**
¹/₄ cup finely diced bell peppers
²/₃ cup finely diced onions
¹/₄ cup ground Westphalian ham or prosciutto**
¹/₄ cup ground ordinary ham
³/₄ cup bread crumbs
¹/₄ cup cream
¹/₄ cup freshly grated Parmesan cheese
¹/₄ teaspoon freshly grated black pepper
Splash of Worcestershire sauce
2 tablespoons Madeira wine

· · · · · ·

Wash the mushroom caps and set aside. Put the other mushrooms, including the stems, in the bowl of the food processor. Process until finely chopped.

Put the slices of bacon in a heavy-bottom sauté pan and cook until crisp. Remove and drain on paper towels. Crumble and reserve. Cook the mushrooms in the bacon fat, adding the onion and bell pepper. Cook until all the moisture has evaporated. Add the ham and the cooked, crumbled bacon and sauté for 5 minutes, stirring to blend.

Preheat oven to 325 degrees. Remove from the heat and add the last 6 ingredients to the ham-mushroom mixture. Stuff the mushroom caps with the mixture and bake for 10-15 minutes. Serve at once. Yield: 12-18 stuffed mushrooms.

* If these are to be hors d'oeuvres, you may want to use smaller mushroom caps for a bite-sized, more easily managed tidbit. You would then need 24-36 small caps.
** If desired, eliminate the bacon and ham to make this dish suitable for vegetarians. Double the amount of Parmesan cheese, cream, and bread crumbs. Use one cup of onions.

In Muscoda, Wisconsin, there is an annual morel mushroom festival, where an entire weekend's activities center around the hunt for this delicious woodland morsel. Some "wild" mushrooms like the shiitake and portabella are now raised commercially in Wisconsin and are readily available year 'round.

This is Quivey's signature hors d'oeuvre. The trout puff is perfect for stand-up parties, since each is one mouthful and can be popped into the mouth neatly with nothing lingering on the fingers.

This pastry, which the French call pâté à choux, may also be filled with a variety of savory or sweet things. The basis for cream puffs and eclairs, it is not difficult to make, the eggs in the recipe causing the mixture to puff up like magic.

Smoked Trout Puffs

Quivey's Grove has made close to a quarter-million of these delectable little puffs. At a popular wedding show each year, the restaurant gives away about seven thousand to prospective brides, grooms, and parents of the bride. Many return for another taste, "just to make sure."

PUFFS	TROUT SALAD
$^1/_2$ cup water	1 pound cleaned, smoked trout
$^1/_2$ cup milk	$^1/_2$ cup finely diced onion
4 ounces butter	1 teaspoon seasoning salt
1 teaspoon salt	2 teaspoons Dijon-style mustard
$1^1/_2$ teaspoons sugar	1 tablespoon cream
1 cup flour	$^1/_2$ cup finely diced celery
5 eggs	1 tablespoon lemon pepper
	1 teaspoon parsley flakes
	2 teaspoons ketchup
	$^2/_3$ cup mayonnaise

For the puffs: Heat the water, milk, butter, salt, and sugar just to a boil. Add the flour all at once and stir with a wooden spoon, cooking over medium heat until the dough forms a large stiff ball. Remove from heat and beat in eggs, one at a time, keeping paste stiff. Grease and flour a baking sheet. Preheat oven to 425 degrees.

Put a half-open tip on a pastry bag and fill bag with the dough. Pipe out little puffs, about 1-inch in diameter and 1-inch high. Bake without disturbing for 10 minutes. Lower heat to 350 and bake another ten minutes until dry, puffed and set.

Mix all the salad ingredients together. Split the puffs, cool them thoroughly, and put a teaspoonful of salad in each. Serve. Yield: about 25 puffs.

To serve large numbers of people, it always helps to have at least one spread or dip for them to eat with crackers, biscuits, small pieces of bread, or fresh vegetables, which the French call crudités. Spreads and dips can stretch your entertaining budget and satisfy people's appetites. They're also easy to prepare, even by those with little kitchen experience.

Spreads and dips are forgiving. If you find yourself short on an ingredient or lack one of the seasonings, substitute something else. Dips and spreads are easy to experiment with. You can introduce variations of your own or intensify flavors that you especially like.

The following Quivey's spreads have stood the test of time, pleasing thousands of patrons of the restaurant and starring at hundreds of catered events.

Bacon, Cheddar & Horsey Spread

2 pounds cream cheese
1/4 pound crisp cooked bacon
1/4 pound clear bacon fat
2 ounces Westphalian ham
2 tablespoons diced shallots
3 tablespoons fresh horseradish*
1 cup grated sharp Cheddar cheese
Salt & pepper to taste
Crumbled cooked bacon
Fresh parsley, stems removed

· · · · · ·

Put all the ingredients into the work bowl of a food processor and process till smooth. Seasonings may be adjusted to suit your taste. Garnish with cooked bacon and fresh parsley.

*Horseradish loses its heat quickly, so use the freshest available. Grating your own is preferred. If buying a commercial product, read the label. Many prepared horseradishes are cut with turnips and are nearly tasteless. They should not be used in a recipe that calls for real horseradish.

Beer was popular in this region long before statehood, the result of a large influx of Germans, especially in the Milwaukee area. The great German brewing families— Miller, Pabst, Schlitz, Blatz—are still big names in beer today. Wisconsin became the dairy state when wheat farming dried up (because of disease). Agricultural experts urged farmers to trade "the plow for the cow" and cheese has been king ever since.

Beer and cheese go together very well, especially with the addition of crackers. Here is a delicious spread, wonderful when used with small rye or pumpernickel rounds.

Beer Cheese Spread

4 cups grated aged Cheddar cheese
8 ounces cream cheese
1 teaspoon Worcestershire sauce
$^1/_2$ teaspoon dry mustard
1 clove garlic
$^1/_2$ cup Wisconsin beer
1 teaspoon onion salt

. . . . . .

Put all ingredients in a food processor and process until smooth. Chill and serve with tiny, sour gherkin pickles.

Gorgonzola Walnut Spread

2 pounds cream cheese
$^1/_2$ pound Gorgonzola cheese
1 cup toasted walnuts*
1 tablespoon mashed garlic
1 tablespoon lemon pepper
2 tablespoons chopped fresh chives
Fresh chives, walnut halves

. . . . . .

Put all except the last two ingredients in a food processor and process until smooth. Chill before serving. Garnish with fresh chives and walnut halves.

* To toast nuts, place in a baking pan and put in a 325 degree oven for 10-15 minutes. When you can smell the nuts toasting, you'll know they're close to being ready.

Roasted Red Pepper Spread

2 pounds cream cheese
4 large red bell peppers, roasted, peeled, seeded & chopped
1 tablespoon minced shallot
1 tablespoon garlic paste
1 teaspoon Tabasco sauce
Salt & pepper to taste

. . . . . .

Put all the ingredients into the bowl of a food processor and blend until smooth. Chill and serve. This spread is especially good with fresh vegetables.

Roasting bell peppers is easy. Cut the pepper in half and brush the outside with oil. Broil until they char. Put them in a plastic bag, seal, and let sit for 10 minutes. Then wash off the charred skin under running water.

Nancy Lynch

Soups

Everyone, no matter how small their household, should start soups with homemade stock. Quivey's has at least one stockpot going on the back of the stove at all times. If this is not practical, you can make beef or chicken stock and refrigerate some of it for short-term use, or freeze it for the longer term.

Starting with the stock, there are endless variations of soup to be made, using vegetables, meats, pastas, and grains. Cream soups include a wonderful array of cheeses, sour cream, crème fraîche, whipping cream, half-and-half, and milk, again combined with vegetables, meats, cheeses, and even nuts.

Here is Alexandre Dumas' recipe for Wooden Leg Soup:

Cut both ends off a beef shinbone, leaving it about a foot long. Put it into a big kettle with good bouillon and a good slice of fresh beef, some cold water. Bring slowly to a boil. Skim. Season with salt and a couple of cloves. Add 24-36 carrots, 12 onions, 12 stalks of celery, 12 turnips, 1 hen, and 2 old partridges. Now take a veal round, about 2 pounds, warm slowly in a pot, and fill with bouillon from the above. Skim off the fat. Add 12 little onions, a few small stalks of celery, add the whole thing to the big kettle and cook about one hour. Correct your seasoning. Skim off all fat again. Put grated stale white of bread into a pot. Add bouillon. Simmer. Put into the tureen for serving, add the cooked vegetables, put the bone on top, pour the bouillon over. Serve very hot.

Dumas was writing his *Grand Dictionaire de Cuisine* at the time that Madison became the capital of Wisconsin and Quivey's Grove was built. His recipes, however, are at least a hundred years older than that.

"Fill your pot to the top . . . with a bouillon that has smiled for 6 or 7 days."

—Alexandre Dumas, noted gourmand and author of the Grand Dictionaire de Cuisine

Beef or Veal Stock

5 pounds of cut-up beef bones
1 large carrot
1 leek (white part), cleaned and trimmed
2-3 ribs celery
1 large onion, peeled
2 cloves garlic, peeled
4 tablespoons tomato paste
1 teaspoon thyme
2 bay leaves
1 teaspoon basil
3-4 sprigs parsley, chopped
1 gallon water

. . . . .

Put the bones in a shallow roasting pan and place the pan in the oven at 350 degrees. Roast till all the bones are well browned. Add the vegetables for the last 20-30 minutes. Put the bones and the vegetables in a large stockpot and cover with water. Add the herbs and tomato paste and bring to a boil. Reduce and simmer for at least 4 hours. The longer it cooks, the richer it will be.

Strain the stock and discard the bones and vegetables. Refrigerate. After refrigeration, the stock may be de-fatted by simply removing the layer of congealed fat on the top. The stock may be frozen for later use.

For veal stock, simply follow the above proportions and procedure, substituting veal bones for beef. Veal makes a lighter-flavored stock, somewhere between beef and chicken.

Chicken Stock

5 pounds of chicken bones
1 large carrot
1 leek (white part), cleaned well
1 large onion
2-3 cloves
2 ribs celery
1 shallot
1 clove garlic, peeled
1 teaspoon thyme
1 bay leaf
2-3 stems parsley, chopped
$^1/_2$ lemon

. . . . . .

Brown the bones in a shallow roasting pan till well browned. Add the vegetables the last 20 minutes. (Before adding the vegetables, insert the cloves into the onion.) Scrape the bones and vegetables into a large stockpot with one gallon of water, deglaze* the roasting pan with a little water (or white wine) and add that to the pot. Add the herbs and lemon and bring the pot to a simmer. Cook, uncovered, for several hours. Check periodically to be sure the liquid does not boil away. If the liquid appears to be evaporating too quickly, turn down the heat and add more water, just to cover the bones.

Strain the stock, discarding the bones and vegetables. Refrigerate. Remove the layer of fat that solidifies on top of the broth. The stock may be frozen for later use.

*To deglaze is to dissolve, with wine, stock, or other liquid, the sediment left in the pan after the meat has roasted.

"A chicken in every pot" used to be a politician's campaign pledge— a promise of prosperity. Chicken did not become popular in America until well into the nineteenth century, and did not become a truly inexpensive entree until after World War II. Now, nearly any pot can have a chicken, and the stock pot can have the bones the next day.

This soup does not use stock, but cooks with a ham bone. This is a good way to use the bone from your New Year's or Easter ham, or you can purchase a ham hock especially for this purpose.

Black Bean Soup

1 cup dried black turtle beans
1 ham bone or ham hock
1 quart water
1 medium onion, chopped
$^1/_4$ teaspoon ground cloves
1 bay leaf
$^1/_2$ teaspoon black pepper
2-3 tablespoons Madeira or sherry

· · · · ·

Wash and pick over beans. Put in a bowl and cover with water to soak overnight.

The next day, drain the beans and put into a large soup pot. Add the ham bone, water, onion, and seasonings. If using a ham hock, trim carefully to remove as much fat as possible. Cover and bring to a boil, lower the heat to a simmer. Skim and discard any foam that forms. Cook, covered, until the beans are tender, approximately one hour. When the beans are tender, remove the bone and the bay leaf and puree the mixture in the food processor. Return pot to the burner and heat through. If the soup is too thick, it may thinned with a little water. If too thin, add a bit of whipping cream.   Just before serving, add the Madeira or sherry, whichever is your preference. Garnish the soup with thin slices of lemon and chopped hard-boiled eggs. Yield: 4 servings.

Carrots make terrific soup and have been seasoned with everything from cinnamon to curry in the process. Here is Quivey's version, which should become a family favorite in no time. A good way to get the kids to eat their carrots.

Creamy Carrot Soup

1 quart chicken stock (page 35)
$^1/_4$ teaspoon white pepper
$^1/_4$ cup chopped onion
$2^1/_2$ cups peeled, chopped carrots
2 tablespoons butter or margarine
4 tablespoons flour
2 cups milk, warmed
$^1/_2$ teaspoon ginger
$^1/_4$ teaspoon cinnamon
$^1/_4$ teaspoon allspice
$^1/_4$ teaspoon nutmeg
$^1/_4$ teaspoon Worcestershire sauce
3 tablespoons grated sharp Cheddar cheese

· · · · · ·

In a large kettle bring the chicken stock to a boil. Add the pepper, onion, and carrots and reduce to a simmer. Cook the carrots at a simmer for 20 minutes or until soft. Remove the carrots and onions and puree with a cup of stock in a blender or food processor.

In a large, heavy-bottom saucepan over low heat, melt the butter and stir in the flour, whisking to smooth. Cook for a few minutes, then slowly add the milk, stirring to blend smoothly. Add the pureed carrots and onions, then the spices, Worcestershire sauce, and cheese. Blend thoroughly and serve immediately. Soup should not come to a simmer. If held and reheated, do so in a double boiler. Yield: 4-6 servings.

Cream of Cauliflower & Broccoli Soup

Edible flowers are a colorful part of today's nouvelle cuisine, but we have been eating flowers since childhood— especially in the form of broccoli and cauliflower. The edible parts of both are the immature flower buds. Mark Twain called cauliflower "cabbage with a college education."

1 quart chicken stock (page 35)
$1/4$ teaspoon black pepper
3 cups finely chopped broccoli and cauliflower
$1/4$ cup chopped onion
2 tablespoons butter or margarine
3-4 tablespoons flour
$1^1/2$ cups milk
$1/2$ cup grated aged, sharp Cheddar cheese
Sherry to taste

. . . . . .

Bring the chicken stock to a boil, add the pepper, broccoli, cauliflower, and onion. Simmer just 10 minutes. Strain and reserve the broth.

In a large heavy-bottom saucepan over low heat, melt the butter or margarine and stir in the flour, whisking to incorporate fully. Cook for a few minutes, stirring often. Add the hot broth, whisking to keep the mixture smooth but fairly thick. Slowly add the milk, then the Cheddar cheese, a little at a time, stirring until it melts. Add the sherry, then the reserved vegetables. Serve as soon as the vegetables are heated through. Yield: 10-12 servings.

Some recipes call for the meat for goulash soup to be browned in chicken fat because of the subtle difference in the flavor it brings to the soup. Quivey's has always used bacon fat. And for home preparation, butter and margarine remain suitable options.

Goulash Soup

1 cup sliced onion
1 tablespoon paprika
$^1/_4$ teaspoon minced garlic
3 tablespoons bacon fat or butter
1 pound pork, cut in 1-inch cubes
2 tablespoons flour
$1^1/_2$ quarts beef stock, warmed
$^1/_4$ cup tomato paste
$^1/_4$ teaspoon sugar
$^2/_3$ cup diced tomatoes in juice, seeded and skinned
Salt & pepper to taste
$^3/_4$ cup cooked noodles or spaetzle (see next page)
Crème fraîche (see next page)

· · · · · ·

Sauté the onions and garlic in the bacon fat or butter with paprika until the onions are golden. Add the pork cubes and stir. Cook for 5-10 minutes, stirring often. Sprinkle the flour over the pork and onions, and stir to blend in. Add all the warmed beef stock, a little at a time. Add the tomato paste. Add in the tomatoes and sprinkle the sugar over all. Salt and pepper, cover, and let simmer for 1 hour.

When meat is tender, add the cooked noodles or spaetzle, garnish with crème fraîche, and serve. Chopped green onion or chopped chives look good on the crème fraîche. Yield: 6 servings.

Spaetzle

3¹/₂ cups flour   1 cup milk
¹/₂ teaspoon nutmeg   4 eggs, beaten
2 teaspoons salt

. . . . .

Mix flour, salt, and nutmeg in bowl. Mix eggs and milk, add flour until batter is soft. Pour batter into colander with holes at least ³/₁₆-inch in diameter (or spaetzle maker) and press through holes into boiling, salted water. Stir and cook 5 minutes. Drain well. Yield: 8-10 servings.

Crème Fraîche

2 cups whipping cream
1 tablespoon buttermilk or yogurt

. . . . .

Put the cream in a glass or stainless steel bowl and mix in the buttermilk or yogurt. Allow to stand overnight, unrefrigerated but away from heat sources, lightly covered with a clean dishcloth. The cream should have thickened. This is what the French call crème fraîche and it's useful for cooking as well as delicious with fresh berries in the summer.

The Scots cook a lot of lamb and mutton. And because they have a reputation for thrift, not to say stinginess, they use every part of the sheep. One of their national dishes, haggis, involves oatmeal and a sheep's stomach. However, much can be forgiven a people who make single-malt Scotch whisky and lamb broth with barley.

Scottish Lamb Broth

2 pounds lamb shanks
2 tablespoons oil
2 cloves garlic
2 carrots, peeled & chopped
1 small onion, chopped
1 rib celery, chopped
1 tomato, chopped
2 cups red wine
6 cups water
1 sprig rosemary
1 teaspoon thyme
1 teaspoon pepper
$^1/_2$ cup barley

. . . . . .

In a cast-iron Dutch oven, brown the lamb shanks well on all sides in the oil. Remove. Add the vegetables and brown well. Add the shanks, liquids, and seasonings and bring to a boil. Reduce to a simmer and cook till lamb is tender, skimming off any scum that forms. Let the shanks cool in the broth and remove. Skim all fat from the top of the stock. Reheat the soup and add the barley. Simmer until the barley is tender. Remove the meat from the shanks and chop. Add back to the pot. Adjust seasonings to taste and serve with hearty bread and good butter. Yield: 6-8 servings.

Sheep are not a popular livestock animal on Wisconsin farms, accounting for only about 100,000 head throughout the state, a mere 1% of the nation's total. The leading U.S. sheep producer is Texas, and many Wisconsin restaurants now import lamb from New Zealand.

This soup was originally developed at the restaurant to use up leftover pork roast. It makes a delicious, warming winter soup for home as well.

Creamy Pork & Cider Soup

2 small onions, diced
1 apple, peeled, cored, and diced
2 tablespoons butter
2-3 cups cubed & cooked pork
3 cups peeled & cubed potatoes
2 quarts chicken stock
1 cup cider
2 cups half-and-half
2 tablespoons butter, softened
3 tablespoons flour
$^1/_4$ cup apple brandy
Pinch of salt, or to taste
Pinch of white pepper
$^1/_4$ teaspoon nutmeg
$^1/_4$ teaspoon allspice

. . . . .

Melt the butter in a heavy-bottom soup pot. Cook the onions and apple in the butter until they soften, but do not brown. Add the potatoes and pork and stir to coat.

Add the chicken stock, cider and cream. Bring to a boil and reduce to a simmer. Cook until the potatoes are tender. Thicken the soup if necessary with a roux made from softened butter mixed with flour. Add the apple brandy and seasonings, adjusting to taste. Serve. Garnish with fresh chopped chives. Yield: 6-8 servings.

This recipe for tomato soup is the one chosen by Sally A. C. Wood, curator of interpretation at the Wade House in Greenbush, Wisconsin, for use at their harvest suppers. The Wade House was a stagecoach inn in the 1850s and so was in operation at the time Quivey's Grove was built. Contrast this recipe with the one currently in use at Quivey's (next page) to see how a contemporary chef adapts traditional recipes for the modern palate.

Tomato Cream Soup

4 cups canned tomatoes
1 medium onion, peeled & chopped
2 ribs celery, finely chopped
4 cups scalded milk
About one tablespoon flour to thicken 2 tablespoons water
$^1/_2$ teaspoon baking soda
1 tablespoon butter
Salt & pepper to taste

. . . . . .

Simmer tomatoes, onion, and celery for 30 minutes over low heat. Meanwhile, scald the milk and thicken slightly with the flour mixed with water to make a smooth paste. Just before serving, add the soda to the tomatoes and as frothing subsides, strain into the hot milk, stirring constantly (the soda prevents curdling). Add butter, then salt and pepper. Serve at once. Yield: 5-6 servings.

This recipe may be doubled, but do not increase the amount of soda.

Here is Quivey's fresh tomato soup. See if using fresh garden tomatoes doesn't make all the difference in both taste and texture. A wonderful early September luncheon can be planned around this soup.

Fresh Tomato Soup

8 tablespoons butter or margarine
2 tablespoons water
2 medium onions, finely sliced
2 cloves garlic, chopped
2 cloves shallot, chopped
1 cup fresh basil leaves, loosely packed
1 sprig rosemary, de-stemmed
1 teaspoon sugar
2 pounds ripe tomatoes, washed, cored, seeded, and
    chopped
3 cups whipping cream
2 egg yolks

· · · · · ·

Melt the butter over low heat, add the water. Add the onions, garlic, and shallot and cook until soft but not browned. Chop the basil coarsely and add to the onion mixture. Add the rosemary. Add the tomatoes, sprinkle the sugar over them, and cook just to heat and soften. Puree in the food processor and strain. Return the puree to the heat. Mix the cream and egg yolks. Heat the puree just to a boil and add in the well-beaten cream mix. Heat the mixture to about 165 degrees. DO NOT boil or the soup will "break" or curdle. Soup should be slightly thickened.

Garnish each serving with a dollop of sour cream or yogurt and a sprig of fresh basil. Yield: Serves 6-8.

Here is one of Craig's own recipes. Turkey Soup with Dumplings is served at the restaurant after Thanksgiving and Christmas, but this is the recipe that Craig uses at home for his family and guests.

Turkey Soup with Dumplings

1 turkey carcass, broken up
3 medium onions, chopped
4 medium carrots, cut in chunks
6 peppercorns
4 cloves
1 teaspoon thyme
1 gallon water, approximately
2 tablespoons turkey fat, reserved from roasting pan
1 onion, diced
2 ribs celery, diced

DUMPLINGS
1 cup flour
Pinch nutmeg
$1/2$ teaspoon salt
$1/4$ cup milk
1 egg

. . . . . .

Pick all the meat off the carcass and set aside to be added to the soup later. Put the turkey carcass in a large stockpot with 2 onions, 2 carrots, and spices. Cover with water and bring to a boil. Reduce to a simmer and cover. Simmer 4 hours, skimming the scum off occasionally. Strain broth and cool. Refrigerate broth and then skim the fat off the top.

Dice and sauté the remaining vegetables in the reserved turkey fat until they are soft. Add to the broth along with reserved turkey meat.

For the dumplings: Mix the flour, nutmeg, and salt together. Beat the milk and egg together. Stir the flour into the milk mixture. Beat just until a soft dough forms.

"In Wisconsin, the earliest record of wild turkeys was in 1670 when the Jesuit Allouez noted turkeys in the Lake Winnebago area. Later records indicate that turkeys were abundant south of a line from Green Bay to Prairie du Chien. In 1856 [the year after Quivey's was built] wild turkeys sold for 25 cents apiece around Lancaster."

—Tim Eisele, in
The Wisconsin
Almanac, *1989*

Bring the soup to a boil. Dip 2 spoons into broth. Scoop dumpling mixture in one spoon and with the other cut off little bits of dough, dropping them into the boiling soup. Repeat until you've used all the dough. Dumplings are done and the soup is ready to serve when the dumplings float. Don't make them large. Yield: one ample pot of turkey soup.

Finally, here's a quick but elegant soup that's good for company or for a rainy day in spring. Excellent served with a good, chilled, dry Chardonnay, crusty bread, and a tossed green salad.

Smoked Trout Soup

1 small onion, diced
1 carrot, diced
2 tablespoons butter
1 medium potato, peeled, boiled & diced
6 ounces smoked trout, boneless & skinless, broken into
    chunks
2 cups half-and-half
$^1/_2$ teaspoon thyme
Salt & pepper to taste

. . . . . .

In a heavy-bottom soup pot, sweat the onion and carrot in the butter without browning. Add the potato and the trout and stir to coat with the butter. Slowly add the half-and-half and thyme. Heat, but do not allow soup to boil. Adjust the seasonings with salt and pepper. Garnish with parsley or crumbled bacon. Yield: 4 servings.

Nancy Lynch

Muffins

Quivey's Grove is famous for its piping hot, right-from-the-oven muffins that come wrapped in a fresh napkin, served in a basket, and accompanied by plenty of good Wisconsin butter. In fifteen years the restaurant has served nearly a half-million muffins.

One of the dividends of having a private party at Quivey's is that you might come home with the muffins left over from your gathering—indeed, if there are any left over. You can also request a favorite muffin in advance, and the staff will do their best to accommodate your tastes.

There are a few bakers' tricks that you can use to make better muffins. One is to use buttermilk instead of regular milk. Most serious bakers prefer buttermilk because it gives a better rise to the batter, adds a little kick to the flavor, and improves the texture. Buttermilk is lower in fat and cholesterol as well. You may also substitute your favorite yogurt for milk, although yogurts have widely differing consistencies and may produce unpredictable results. But you may experiment in this area, if you wish.

Also, if you bring the eggs and fat or oil to room temperature, you'll find that your muffins bake up lighter.

Another trick to help your muffins reach impressive heights is to preheat the oven to a temperature 50 degrees higher than is called for in the recipe. When you put the muffin tins in the oven, lower the setting to the recommended temperature.

One final hint: when mixing the wet ingredients with the dry, don't over-mix. All the ingredients should be moist and the batter may be lumpy. Lumpy batter is definitely okay when it comes to muffins.

Occasionally, these muffins are made with apples from the tree outside the Stable Tap. The lone tree, however, cannot supply enough to satisfy the patrons' demand for these delectable muffins.

Apple Muffins

$^1/_4$ cup butter or margarine, softened
6 tablespoons sugar
$^1/_4$ cup brown sugar
1 egg
$^1/_2$ cup buttermilk
$^1/_2$ cup apple cider
2 cups sifted flour
1 teaspoon baking soda
$^1/_4$ teaspoon baking powder
1 teaspoon cinnamon
$^1/_8$ teaspoon allspice
$^3/_4$ cup finely chopped apples

Preheat oven to 375 degrees. Place paper liners in 12 muffin cups.

Cream together the butter or margarine and sugars until light and fluffy. Add in the egg and mix well. Combine buttermilk and cider. Sift flour, adding baking soda, powder, and spices. Add flour mixture to the sugar mixture alternately with the buttermilk and cider mixture. When all the ingredients have been lightly blended, add the chopped apples. Spoon into muffin tins, sprinkle with brown sugar, and put into the oven.

Bake for 18 to 20 minutes or until tops are lightly browned. Serve piping hot. Yield: 12 muffins.

Banana Nut Muffins

$^1/_4$ cup butter or margarine, softened
6 tablespoons sugar
$^1/_4$ cup brown sugar
1 egg
$^2/_3$ cup mashed, ripe* banana
1 cup buttermilk
2 cups sifted flour
1 teaspoon baking soda
$^1/_4$ teaspoon baking powder
$^1/_8$ teaspoon allspice
$^1/_3$ cup chopped walnuts

Preheat oven to 375 degrees. Place paper liners in 12 muffin cups.

Cream butter or margarine with the sugars until light and fluffy. Add the egg and mix well. Combine buttermilk with banana and mix well till smooth. Sift the flour, adding baking soda, powder, and allspice. Alternately add the flour mixture and banana mixture to sugar mixture until all the ingredients are incorporated. Add nuts, spoon the batter into muffin cups, and sprinkle with brown sugar.

Bake 18-20 minutes or until the muffins are lightly browned on top. Serve at once. Yield: 12 muffins.

*The riper the banana, the stronger the flavor; the skin can be perfectly black and the banana inside will be full of flavor and perfect for bread or muffins.

The best blueberries are the small wild ones, full of intense flavor. They are found up north in Wisconsin just as they are in northern New England. Their commercial counterparts are not nearly as flavorful but will still make a good muffin. If you can go berrying up north, though, do take advantage and make these muffins, tasting the difference for yourself. You can occasionally find the small wild ones canned in water from Maine. Those can be used in these muffins, too, if they are thoroughly drained.

Blueberry Muffins

$^1/_4$ cup butter or margarine, softened
$^1/_2$ cup + 2 tablespoons sugar
1 egg
1 cup buttermilk
2 cups sifted flour
1 teaspoon baking soda
$^1/_4$ teaspoon baking powder
$^1/_8$ teaspoon nutmeg
$^3/_4$ cup blueberries

Preheat oven to 375 degrees. Place paper liners in 12 muffin cups.

Cream the butter or margarine with sugar until fluffy. Add the egg and mix well. Sift the flour, adding baking soda, baking powder, and nutmeg. Add alternately with the buttermilk to the sugar mixture until all ingredients are incorporated. Gently fold in the blueberries, spoon batter into the cups, and sprinkle with white granulated sugar.

Bake 18-20 minutes or until the tops are lightly browned. Serve hot. Yield: 12 muffins.

This recipe may be used also for strawberry and cherry muffins. Simply substitute $^3/_4$ cup chopped fresh strawberries or $^3/_4$ cup chopped cherries.

Savory rather than sweet muffins are an interesting varia-tion and one that can easily move to the dinner table at home. Surprise friends and family with this one, or try the onion muffins. Serve both for a large family dinner.

Caraway Cheddar Muffins

$^1/_4$ cup butter or margarine, softened
2 tablespoons + 2 teaspoons sugar
1 egg
1 cup buttermilk
$1^3/_4$ cups sifted flour
1 teaspoon baking soda
$^1/_4$ teaspoon baking powder
$^1/_4$ teaspoon salt
1 teaspoon caraway seed (2, if you like caraway)
4 ounces grated Cheddar cheese
Paprika

· · · · · ·

Preheat oven to 375 degrees. Place paper liners in 12 muffin cups.

Cream margarine with sugar until fluffy. Add the egg, mix-ing well. Sift the flour and add baking soda, powder, salt, and caraway seed. Add the flour mixture alternately to the sugar mixture with the buttermilk until all ingredients are lightly blended. Fold in Cheddar cheese, sprinkle the pap-rika on tops of muffins, and spoon the batter into cups.

Bake 18-20 minutes or until tops are lightly browned. Serve hot. Yield: 12 muffins.

"The controversy over whether to permit the sale of colored oleomargarine in Wisconsin was hard fought. One of those who sought to protect the dairy industry by opposing its sale was Senator Gordon Roselip of Darlington. 'If you pass this bill,' he warned his colleagues, 'you will never be able to look a cow in the face again!'"

—The Wisconsin Almanac, *1989*

Lemon and poppyseeds seem to go together the way peanut butter and jelly do. The combination appears in many recipes for all kinds of baked goods. Here's one of the best, a breakfast indulgence.

Lemon Poppyseed Muffins

$^1/_4$ cup butter or margarine, softened
$^1/_2$ cup + 2 tablespoons sugar
1 egg
1 tablespoon lemon juice
1 teaspoon grated lemon zest
1 cup buttermilk
2 cups sifted flour
$^1/_4$ cup poppyseeds
1 teaspoon baking soda
$^1/_4$ teaspoon baking powder

. . . . . .

Preheat oven to 375 degrees. Place paper liners in 12 muffin cups.

Cream butter or margarine with sugar until fluffy. Add the egg, blending well. Blend buttermilk with lemon juice and rind, and mix well. Sift the flour, adding poppyseeds, baking soda and powder. Add this mixture alternately with the buttermilk mixture to the sugar mixture until all ingredients are lightly blended. Spoon into muffin cups, sprinkle with white granulated sugar, and put in the oven.

Bake for 18-20 minutes or until tops are lightly browned. Serve hot. Yield: 12 muffins.

Orange juice concentrate is one of the best things to happen to baking in some time. Using it undiluted gives baked goods like muffins rich orange flavor with little effort on your part.

Orange Cranberry Muffins

$^1/_4$ cup butter or margarine, softened
$^1/_2$ cup + 2 tablespoons sugar
1 egg
1 cup buttermilk
2 tablespoons undiluted orange juice concentrate
2 cups flour
1 teaspoon baking soda
$^1/_4$ teaspoon baking powder
$^1/_4$ teaspoon nutmeg
1 cup chopped cranberries

. . . . .

Preheat oven to 350 degrees. Place paper liners in 12 muffin cups. Wash and pick over the cranberries, discarding any discolored ones. Chop enough to make 1 cup.

Cream butter or margarine with sugar until fluffy. Add the egg and beat well. Mix the buttermilk with orange juice concentrate and add into the butter mixture, blending well. Sift flour with baking soda and powder. Add the wet ingredients to the dry, blend well, fold in the cranberries, spoon into the muffin cups, and sprinkle with white granulated sugar.

Bake for 18-20 minutes or until the tops are golden brown. Serve at once. Yield: 12 muffins.

Although pecans are strongly associated with the South, they are also native to the region just a little south of Wisconsin and still grow wild in southern Iowa and Missouri along the Mississippi river.

Orange Pecan Muffins

$^1/_4$ cup butter or margarine, softened
$^1/_2$ cup + 2 tablespoons sugar
1 egg
$^1/_2$ cup + 2 tablespoons buttermilk
6 tablespoons orange juice concentrate
2 cups sifted flour
1 teaspoon baking soda
$^1/_4$ teaspoon baking powder
$^1/_3$ cup chopped pecans

Preheat oven to 375 degrees. Place paper liners in 12 muffin cups.

Cream butter or margarine with sugar until fluffy. Add the egg, mixing well. Blend together the buttermilk and orange juice concentrate. Sift flour, adding baking soda and powder. Alternately add the flour mixture and buttermilk mixture to the sugar mixture until all ingredients are incorporated. Fold in pecans, spoon the batter into the muffin cups, and sprinkle with white granulated sugar.

Put the pan in the oven and bake 18-22 minutes or until the tops are light golden brown. Serve. Yield: 12 muffins.

Onion Muffins

¹/₄ cup butter or margarine
¹/₂ cup chopped onions
1 egg
³/₄ teaspoon Tabasco sauce
1 cup buttermilk
2 tablespoons sugar
2 cups sifted flour
1 teaspoon black pepper
1 teaspoon baking soda
¹/₈ teaspoon baking powder
¹/₄ teaspoon salt

. . . . . .

Preheat oven to 375 degrees. Place paper liners in 12 muffin cups.

Sauté onions in butter or margarine. Beat the egg, add buttermilk and Tabasco, add into the sautéed onions. Sift the flour, adding in the pepper, baking soda, powder, and salt. Add the dry ingredients to the onion mixture, stirring just until all ingredients are blended. Spoon the batter into the muffin cups and sprinkle with just a little paprika.

Bake for 18-20 minutes or until tops are lightly browned. Serve hot. Yield: 12 muffins.

THE MISSING LINK

Evolutionists say
   that our
Race has been
   crossed,
And in the great
   chain
One link had got
   lost.
But now that's
   exploded,
Your face, and
   your shape
Show the great
   missing link
Between man and
   the ape.

Oh! what a
   sensation
You'd make at the
   zoo!
What a stare and
   a scare
You would cause at
   a view!
What a great
   creature
For Barnum's
   menagerie!
Another "What is
   it"
For fools to go see!

Peach Muffins

Turn peach, orange, pecan, or berry muffins into a great dessert. Just slice them warm, cut them in half, and top with vanilla ice cream!

$^1/_4$ cup butter or margarine, softened
6 tablespoons sugar
$^1/_4$ cup brown sugar
1 egg
$^3/_4$ cup buttermilk
$^1/_4$ cup peach nectar
2 cups sifted flour
1 teaspoon baking soda
$^1/_4$ teaspoon baking powder
$^1/_8$ teaspoon ground cloves
$^3/_4$ cup chopped fresh or frozen peaches

. . . . .

Preheat oven to 375 degrees. Place paper liners in 12 muffin cups.

Cream butter or margarine with sugars until fluffy. Add the egg and mix well. Blend buttermilk with the peach nectar thoroughly. Sift flour, adding baking soda, powder, and ground cloves. Alternately add the flour mixture with the buttermilk mixture to the sugar mixture until all ingredients are blended. Fold in peaches, spoon the batter into the muffin cups, and sprinkle with white granulated sugar.

Bake for 18-20 minutes or until tops are lightly browned. Serve hot. Yield: 12 muffins.

Quivey's popovers are almost as famous as their muffins. They are always served split sideways and filled, usually with beef or lamb stew, or chicken with mushrooms in a cream sauce. You can serve these popovers that way, or you can serve them just as you would the muffins, in a napkin-lined basket with plenty of good Wisconsin butter to accompany them.

Craig has discovered that if the batter is made up the day before, refrigerated, and used the next day, the popovers will bake up much lighter and higher.

In James Beard's American Cookery, *the author says that these are strictly American and not a derivative of Yorkshire pudding. He also advocates putting them in a cold oven and turning it to 425 degrees, which might have the same effect as refrigerating the batter overnight. Try it both ways and see which works best. You can also cook them the standard way and see which of the three methods works best for you.*

Popovers

2 eggs
1 cup flour, sifted
Pinch salt
1 cup milk
2 tablespoons canola oil

. . . . . .

Beat the eggs well. Beat in flour and salt. Add the milk, beating to make a smooth batter. Add the oil and beat again. Refrigerate.

Preheat oven to 425 degrees. Grease tins for 12 muffins. Pour the batter into tins, place in the oven, and bake for 30 to 35 minutes. Yield: 12 popovers.

Pumpkin Raisin Muffins

"We have pumpkins at morning and pumpkins at noon,

If it were not for pumpkins we would soon be undoon."

—17th century rhyme, reflecting upon the abundance of pumpkins in the new world

$^1/_4$ cup butter or margarine, softened
3 tablespoons sugar
$^1/_4$ cup brown sugar
2 tablespoons molasses
1 egg
$^3/_4$ cup + 1 tablespoon buttermilk
6 ounces ($^2/_3$ cup) canned pumpkin*
2 cups sifted flour
1 teaspoon baking soda
$^1/_4$ teaspoon baking powder
$^1/_8$ teaspoon ginger
$^1/_8$ teaspoon allspice
$^1/_8$ teaspoon nutmeg
$^1/_3$ cup raisins

Preheat oven to 375 degrees. Place paper liners in 12 muffin cups.

Beat butter or margarine with the sugars until fluffy. Add the molasses. Add the egg, beating well. Sift the flour, adding in baking soda, powder, and spices. Alternately add the flour mixture with the buttermilk to the sugar mixture until all ingredients have been incorporated. Fold in the raisins, spoon the batter into the muffin cups, and sprinkle with brown sugar.

Bake for 18-20 minutes or until tops are lightly browned. Serve hot. Yield: 12 muffins.

* If you wish to use fresh pumpkin, first cut up the pumpkin and scrape the insides free of seeds and strings. Put the chunks in a vegetable steamer and simmer over boiling water until the pumpkin is easily pierced with a fork. Cook and scrape the pumpkin from the skin, discarding skin.

In a just world, Wisconsin would be known as well for its berries as for its cheese. Our cool weather gives a sharp tang to bush fruits, making them prized for cooking and simply for eating fresh, in season. Try this recipe during Wisconsin's long raspberry season. (There are both red and black raspberries, but red ones make the prettiest muffins.)

Raspberry Muffins

2 eggs
2 cups buttermilk
4 ounces butter, melted
4¹/₂ cups flour
1¹/₄ cups sugar
2 teaspoons baking soda
¹/₂ teaspoon salt
¹/₂ teaspoon allspice
2 cups fresh raspberries

. . . . . .

Preheat oven to 425 degrees. Grease 24 muffin cups or line with paper liners.

Beat the eggs with the buttermilk, add the melted butter, blending well. Sift flour, sugar, baking soda, salt, and allspice together. Add half of the dry ingredients to the buttermilk mixture. Stir to blend, add the remaining dry ingredients, again stirring just to blend. Gently fold in the raspberries. Spoon into the muffin cups and sprinkle with granulated white sugar.

Bake 18-22 minutes or until lightly browned. Yield: 24 muffins.

Nancy Lynch

Salads & Salad Dressings

S alad, despite its contemporary image, has a long and most honorable history. Alexandre Dumas, bon vivant and gourmand, as well as author of *The Three Musketeers*, loved to entertain. In a letter accompanying the manuscript of his *Dictionary of Cuisine*, he described how he made salad for his guests:

> First I put the ingredients into the salad bowl, then overturn them onto a platter. Into the empty bowl I put one hard boiled egg yolk for each two persons—six for a dozen guests. These I mash with oil to form a paste, to which I add chervil, crushed tuna, macerated anchovies, Maille mustard, a large spoonful of soya, chopped gherkins, and the chopped white of the eggs. I thin this mixture by stirring in the finest vinegar obtainable. Finally I put the salad back in the bowl, and my servant tosses it. On the tossed salad I sprinkle a pinch of paprika, which is the Hungarian red pepper.

Dumas also categorized the ingredients of a salad, which in his day included chicory, sorrel, lettuce, chard, spinach, and purslane. To this he advocated the use of seasoning herbs: parsley, tarragon, chervil, scallions, shallots, savory, fennel, thyme, sweet basil, and tansy. Garnishing herbs included chives, watercress, and burnet, as well as most of the seasoning herbs.

Not much had changed by the 1950s when this appeared in *Cooking American*:

Young Greens Salad, Putnam County, Connecticut
Watercress, tender leaves or flowers of young dandelions, baby spinach, chicory, sorrel, sliced young radishes, or bits of crisp

lettuce, endive escarole, or romaine may be used. Wash and dry greens with care in very cold water, arrange in salad bowl with a few slices of scallions or mild Spanish onions on sides, and toss them with French dressing. If raw onion is taboo, use slices of hard-cooked egg. Walnut or pecan meats can be sprinkled over top as garnish.

When the spring greens are gone, substitute for them slices of cucumber, chunks of tomato, strips of green pepper, and even nasturtium blossoms with a few of the meaty buds sliced. Toss them in a bowl rubbed with garlic. The fashion of edible flowers is not new but simply revivified. Edible flowers were in use around the turn of this century and perhaps before that.

We have refined the green tossed salad from Dumas' day and simplified the dressing, and we do use different ingredients to vary what is basically an oil and vinegar combination. If using a wooden bowl, some of us still rub the bowl with a clove of garlic before mixing the salad. (And, fewer of us ask our servants to toss the salad!)

Quivey's offers several different vinaigrettes as well as other dressings which have a base of sour cream or buttermilk combined with various cheeses. This is the dairy state, after all, and crisp greens are wonderfully complemented by a dressing made with an authoritative cheese.

There are also salads with a main ingredient of a grilled or sautéed meat, some of which have become popular recently as luncheon entrees. Quivey's Grove also offers salads that are distinctive interpretations of traditional dishes such as chicken and potato salad. These dishes have a history almost as long as the green, tossed salad. Potato salad is made in some countries using oil with lemon juice or vinegar as the dressing. Mayonnaise is a later invention. What we know today as chicken salad was called chicken mayonnaise at the turn of the century. Victorian picnics were far more elaborate than ours are today. They often ran to six or seven courses, culminating with a large assortment of elaborately decorated cakes.

Try some of these recipes of Quivey's for your Fourth of July picnics or Labor Day barbecues.

Asparagus Salad
with Lemon Dijon Dressing

2 pounds asparagus   2 lemons

. . . . . .

Wash and trim the asparagus. Put a pot of water on to boil. Plunge the cleaned asparagus into the boiling water. Boil just until asparagus turns bright green but remains tender—crisp and crunchy (approximately 4 minutes, depending on thickness of stalks). Remove immediately and plunge the asparagus into ice water to refresh. Drain the spears well and place them in the dressing to marinate.

While the asparagus marinates, wash and slice the lemons. Trim each slice and make small scallops in the rind with a sharp knife. Push 5 or 6 spears of asparagus through each lemon slice and arrange the slices on a platter. This will serve 4. Simply increase the amount of asparagus to serve more.

Lemon Dijon Dressing

²/₃ cup olive oil
1 tablespoon Dijon-style mustard
5 tablespoons fresh lemon juice
1 tablespoon finely minced green onion
1 large garlic clove, crushed
Pinch salt
Freshly ground black pepper to taste
1 teaspoon dill weed

. . . . . .

Gently beat the mustard and lemon juice into the oil. Add the other ingredients and continue beating until all ingredients are well incorporated. Taste to correct seasonings. Serve on the asparagus. This dressing is also good when used on fresh greens.

Asparagus is one of the most prized crops of the early spring Wisconsin garden. It takes three years to establish a bed of asparagus, but, once established, the bed should produce for a lifetime. Seldom is a single planting so well rewarded in the garden!

Chicken Salad

SALAD
3 cups diced, cooked chicken
³/₄ cup diagonally sliced celery
³/₄ cup chunks red apple, unpeeled
¹/₄ cup pineapple chunks, reserve juice
¹/₄ cup raisins
¹/₄ cup chopped walnuts
¹/₄ cup pineapple juice

DRESSING
3 tablespoons whipping cream
³/₄ cup mayonnaise
1 teaspoon curry powder
¹/₄ teaspoon white pepper or to taste
1 teaspoon salt
¹/₄ cup pineapple juice
1 small clove garlic, mashed

· · · · ·

If you don't have leftover chicken, gently poach several pieces of chicken for 15-20 minutes in simmering water to which you have added a bay leaf, several peppercorns, and an onion stuck with cloves. Remove the chicken and save the strained broth for another use. When the chicken is cool, peel and de-bone, then dice into 1-inch cubes.

Prepare the dressing. Put all ingredients in a small bowl and beat well until thoroughly mixed.

Put all the salad ingredients in a large bowl and toss gently to mix.

Pour the dressing over the salad ingredients slowly, using just enough to thoroughly moisten the ingredients without drowning them. Mix well, cover, and put the salad in the refrigerator for two hours or overnight. Serves 4.

Remember that any salad containing meat or eggs should be kept refrigerated, or chilled on ice for picnics. It is not likely that the mayonnaise will spoil—mayonnaise contains both vinegar and lemon juice which are natural preservatives—but the meat and eggs can easily spoil.

If you'd like to serve this in a traditional way, select 4 ripe tomatoes of about the same size and hollow them out. Heap the chicken salad into the tomato "bowls" and serve them on a bed of attractive greens. Or cut the tomatoes in 8 wedges, leaving them attached at the blossom end. Place on a bed of greens and heap the chicken salad on top. The wedges should look like the spokes of a wheel.

Grilled Chicken & Vegetable Salad

SALAD
4 boned and skinned
  chicken breasts
2 small zucchini
2 small yellow squash
6 large mushrooms
2 small red onions
1 red bell pepper
1 green bell pepper
6 cups cleaned, torn
  romaine lettuce

DRESSING
1 cup red wine vinegar
$^1/_3$ cup balsamic vinegar
$1^1/_3$ cups olive oil
4 cloves garlic, crushed
1 tablespoon black pepper
1 tablespoon minced fresh
  rosemary
2 tablespoons minced fresh
  basil
1 tablespoon sugar

Mix the dressing ingredients together. Put the chicken in a non-reactive (glass or stainless steel) shallow dish and pour a half cup of the dressing over the breasts. Marinate in the refrigerator for 2 hours.

Cut the zucchini and yellow squash in half the short way, then in half the long way. Peel and trim the red onions, leaving the root end on. Cut each into quarters. Clean and seed the peppers, cutting each into eight strips. Marinate the vegetables with one cup of the dressing in the refrigerator for 1 hour. Light the grill.

Heat the remaining cup and a half of dressing to warm and hold. Drain and grill the chicken breasts over medium coals till tender. Reserve and keep warm. Drain and grill the vegetables.

Mound lettuce in the center of 4 plates. Slice zucchini and yellow squash into bite-size pieces and place in center of lettuce. Arrange the remainder of the vegetables around the lettuce. Slice the chicken breasts and arrange the slices over the salad. Ladle some of the warm dressing over each and serve. Yield: 4 servings.

In this recipe you can substitute sour half-and-half for the sour cream to reduce calories and fat without sacrificing flavor. Several of our home cook recipe testers commented that this salad reminded them of ones their mothers or grandmothers served. One tester also reminded cooks to taste each cucumber before adding it to the sour cream. She got one that was bitter and nearly ruined her salad. Variations of this recipe can be found in many old cookbooks.

Cucumbers in Sour Cream

2¹/₂ pounds cucumbers, peeled, de-seeded, and sliced
1 cup sour cream
¹/₄ cup minced onion
1 garlic clove, minced
¹/₄ teaspoon celery salt
1 teaspoon dill
¹/₂ teaspoon chopped fresh chives
1 teaspoon fresh lemon juice

· · · · · ·

Peel the cucumbers if the skin is tough. (If the cucumbers are young and smooth, you can simply score the skins lengthwise with a fork and slice them.) Once peeled or scored, cut in half lengthwise and remove the seeded center section, then slice. Put the sliced cucumbers in a colander, salt lightly, toss, and allow to drain for at least ¹/₂ hour. Squeeze dry before dressing is added.

Prepare the dressing, blending all the ingredients well. Pour over cucumbers and stir to coat all the slices with dressing. These may be held in the refrigerator for several hours before serving. Serves 6-8.

Duck yields a rich, dark meat that is perfect for grilling or sautéing, and takes well to herbs, spices, and fruits.

Duck & Raspberry Salad

RASPBERRY VINAIGRETTE
1/2 cup raspberry vinegar
1 shallot, finely chopped
1 clove garlic, mashed
1 teaspoon salt
1 teaspoon freshly ground black pepper
2 teaspoons sugar
1 1/2 tablespoons sauterne
1 1/2 cups walnut oil

To julienne is to cut into long, narrow strips. (One culinary dictionary makes a comparison to matchsticks.)

SALAD
4 (12-ounce) duck breasts, skinned and boned
1 tablespoon duck fat
1/4 cup toasted walnuts
1/4 cup fine julienne celery
1/4 cup fine julienne green onion
1/2 cup dried cherries
1/2 cup diced apples
1 cup chiffonade Napa cabbage
6 cups cleaned, torn salad greens
1/2 pint fresh raspberries

Mix all the dressing ingredients together except the oil. Slowly beat in the oil till well blended and completely emulsified. Reserve.

Sauté the duck breasts in the duck fat until medium rare. Cool and then julienne. Toss the duck, walnuts, celery, green onion, cherries, and apples together with half the dressing. Reserve the rest of the dressing for another use. Mound the greens on four plates, sprinkle the Napa cabbage on top, then distribute the salad on top of that. Garnish with the fresh raspberries. Yield: 4 salads.

This salad was on Quivey's first menu, and has remained one of their most popular salads through the years. Guests still ask for it today. It's an easy-to-prepare salad for a large group of people, yet very satisfying for only two or four.

Marinated Mushroom Salad

1 cup olive oil
$^1/_4$ cup red wine vinegar
3 tablespoons fresh lemon juice
1 teaspoon minced garlic
2 teaspoons crumbled dried tarragon (or 1$^1/_2$ tablespoons fresh)
1 tablespoon fresh chopped chives
1 tablespoon sugar
1 pound mushrooms, sliced
1 pound spinach
Freshly grated Parmesan cheese
Croutons

. . . . . .

Mix together all the dressing ingredients except the oil, then beat into the oil slowly to emulsify. Clean and slice the mushrooms. Put the mushrooms in a flat, shallow, glass or stainless steel pan and pour the dressing over the mushrooms. Refrigerate for at least an hour, preferably several hours or overnight. Stir once or twice before serving to be sure all the mushrooms are thoroughly marinated.

Clean spinach well under cold, running water. Dry carefully and tear up larger leaves. Put a mound of spinach on each plate, spoon the marinated mushrooms on top, and sprinkle the freshly grated cheese and a few croutons on top. Serve. Yield: 4 salads.

Country Potato Salad

2 pounds red potatoes, cut in quarters
$3/4$ cup carrots, sliced diagonally
$3/4$ cup asparagus, cut in 1-inch pieces*
$3/4$ cup broccoli, cut in 1-inch chunks
$3/4$ cup chopped red onion
$1/2$ cup pepper summer sausage, cut in diamond-shape
     slices
$1/2$ cup Gouda cheese, cut in diamond-shape slices

DRESSING
$1/3$ cup olive or canola oil
3 tablespoons red wine vinegar
Pinch sugar (optional)
1 garlic clove, mashed
Freshly ground pepper to taste
Salt to taste
$1/2$ teaspoon finely chopped chives
1 teaspoon Dijon-style mustard

．．．．．

Wash and quarter the potatoes, and put them on to boil.
When the water comes to a boil, reduce heat and simmer for
10 minutes or so, until the chunks of potato are fork tender
or al dente. Drain. Refresh them under cold water and drain
again.

Blanch the carrots for five minutes, adding the asparagus and
broccoli for the last two minutes. Drain, refresh under cold
water, and drain again.

Mix the dressing ingredients together, blending well. In a large
bowl, put the potatoes, blanched vegetables, onions, sausage,
and cheese. Pour the dressing over all and stir to blend thoroughly. Garnish with sliced hard-boiled eggs. Serves 4-6.

*If asparagus is out of season, simply increase the amount of
broccoli and carrots.

Grilled Sirloin Salad
with Steak Sauce Vinaigrette

SALAD
1 pound sirloin, trimmed of fat
2 small zucchini
2 small yellow squash
8 large mushrooms
2 small red onions
2 red bell peppers
1 green bell pepper
6 cups washed, torn romaine lettuce

DRESSING
1 cup red wine vinegar
$^1/_3$ cup balsamic vinegar
$1^1/_3$ cups olive oil
$^1/_2$ cup steak sauce
4 cloves garlic, crushed
2 teaspoons freshly ground black pepper
6 green onions, finely minced
2 tablespoons Dijon-style mustard

· · · · · ·

Combine all the dressing ingredients except the oil, then slowly mix into the oil. Marinate the sirloin in $^1/_2$ cup of the dressing for two hours. Cut squash in half the short way, and in half again the long way. Peel, trim, and quarter the red onions. Clean and seed peppers, and cut into 8 strips. Marinate the vegetables in 1 cup of the dressing for 1 hour.

Heat $1^1/_2$ cups of the dressing just to warm. Grill the sirloin steak over hot coals till done. Reserve and keep warm. Drain and grill the vegetables over medium coals till done.

Mound the lettuce on 4 plates. Slice squash into bite-size pieces and place in center of lettuce. Arrange remainder of vegetables around the lettuce. Slice the sirloin and arrange the slices over the salad. Ladle some of the warmed dressing over all and serve. Yield: 4 salads.

Zucchini Salad

3-4 zucchini, julienned into 3-inch strips
$1/3$ cup olive or canola oil
$2^1/2$ tablespoons lemon juice
1 teaspoon Dijon-style mustard
1 clove garlic, mashed
1 tablespoon sour cream
1 tablespoon yogurt
Salt & pepper to taste
Chopped parsley and grated radishes
Lettuce, washed and drained

Keep zucchini chilled. Mix together all the ingredients for the dressing and blend well. Pour over the zucchini and toss gently.

Put leaf lettuce on individual plates. Place zucchini on lettuce and sprinkle chopped parsley and grated radish on top. Serve at once. Serves 2-4.

Here are two bacon dressings, the first a traditional recipe and the second—Manny's Bacon Dressing—less traditional, although very rich and just as bacony. Manny is a chef at the Guana Island Club in the British West Indies. He spent a summer cooking at Quivey's Grove and brought his bacon dressing recipe with him.

Hot Bacon Dressing

4 slices good-quality, lean bacon*
Pinch of sugar or to taste
Salt to taste
$^1/_2$ teaspoon dry mustard
$^3/_4$ cup cider vinegar
$^1/_2$ cup canola or good salad oil

· · · · · ·

In a heavy saucepan, cook the bacon until crisp. Remove the slices to a paper towel to drain. Add all the other ingredients to the bacon fat in the pan, keeping the pan on the burner, turned low. Whisk to blend thoroughly and serve.

This dressing is traditional for a spinach-based salad which also incorporates hard-boiled eggs, fresh mushrooms, and the crumbled bacon. Hot bacon dressing should "dress" a salad for 6 to 8 people.

* Cheap bacon will yield too much fat and too little meat for the dressing.

I'm going to Wisconsin and I'm going to stay right there

It sort of peps you up when you breathe Wisconsin air

So I'm going to Wisconsin where I'll live a life of ease

To the land of milk and honey where the money grows on trees

Manny's Bacon Dressing

3 slices good-quality, lean bacon
$^1/_3$ cup sour cream
$^1/_3$ cup good mayonnaise
$^1/_4$ cup red wine
2 tablespoons red wine vinegar
Pinch sugar
1 teaspoon Dijon-style mustard
$^1/_3$ cup finely chopped onions

. . . . . .

Cook the bacon until crisp. Remove and drain on paper towel. Reserve.

Combine all the ingredients except the bacon and refrigerate. When ready to serve the salad, use the dressing and crumble the cooked bacon over all. This should dress a salad for 4-6 people.

Blue Cheese Dressing

$^1/_2$ cup buttermilk
$^1/_2$ cup sour cream*
$^1/_2$ cup crumbled blue cheese
Tabasco sauce, to taste
Pinch of salt
1 teaspoon minced garlic
Freshly cracked black pepper to taste
1 tablespoon chopped fresh chives

. . . . . .

Put the buttermilk, sour cream, and blue cheese in a bowl. Beat with a whisk to combine. Add in the other ingredients and whisk again to combine. If dressing is too thick, it may be thinned, with either a little milk or water.

* Sour half-and-half may be substituted

Cheddar Cheese Dressing

1 cup sour cream or sour half & half
$^1/_3$ cup grated sharp, aged Cheddar cheese
$^1/_3$ cup milk
$^1/_4$ teaspoon fresh lemon juice
Dash Worcestershire sauce
Dash Tabasco sauce
$^1/_4$ teaspoon sugar
$^1/_4$ teaspoon garlic salt
$^1/_4$ cup finely diced onion
$^1/_4$ cup finely chopped chives

. . . . . .

Blend together the sour cream, cheese, and milk till smooth. Add the seasonings and beat well to blend thoroughly. Refrigerate until needed. Serve. Yield: $1^1/_2$ cups of dressing.

California is said to have replaced Wisconsin as the dairy state. But when it comes to making blue cheese, Wisconsin loyalists have nothing to fear. We produce more than 27 million pounds of blue cheese annually—80 percent of the nation's total!

Gorgonzola Dressing

$^1/_2$ cup sour half & half
$^1/_2$ cup half & half
$^1/_4$ cup Gorgonzola cheese
$^1/_2$ teaspoon Tabasco sauce
Pinch salt
1 teaspoon finely minced fresh garlic
Freshly cracked black pepper
1 tablespoon minced fresh chives

. . . . .

Put all ingredients, except the chives, in a blender or food processor. Blend thoroughly. Add the chives, stir gently and use. Or you can hold the chives and sprinkle on top after pouring the dressing over the salad.

Thomas Jefferson was partial to salad and interested in cultivating sesame seed as a substitute for imported olive oil. The following recipe, from the American Heritage Cookbook, *uses the traditional olive oil in combination with sesame oil.*

Monticello Dressing

. . . . .

Combine 1 small clove of garlic (crushed), 1 teaspoon salt, $^1/_2$ teaspoon white pepper, $^1/_3$ cup olive oil, $^1/_3$ cup sesame oil, $^1/_3$ cup tarragon vinegar or wine vinegar. Place in a covered jar and shake well before pouring over salad.

Artichoke Vinaigrette

2-3 artichoke hearts, marinated in oil (do not drain)
$^2/_3$ cup olive oil
3 tablespoons lemon juice
3 tablespoons raspberry vinegar
1 garlic clove, minced
Salt and freshly-ground black pepper to taste

. . . . . .

Put the artichoke hearts and olive oil in a food processor or blender. Process just until blended. Add the other ingredients and whisk gently until well blended. If the dressing is too thick for your taste, it can be thinned with more oil, lemon juice, and vinegar. Remember that the proportions are 3 parts oil to 1 part vinegar.

This vinaigrette is especially good with a shrimp or crabmeat salad.

Shallot Vinaigrette

$^3/_4$ cup olive or good salad oil
1 tablespoon malt vinegar
2 tablespoons cider vinegar
1 tablespoon lemon juice
3-4 shallots, peeled
1 small red onion, peeled and chopped
1 teaspoon lemon pepper
$^1/_4$ teaspoon Tabasco sauce
$^1/_2$ teaspoon fresh horseradish

. . . . . .

Put all the ingredients in a blender or food processor and process just until thoroughly blended. Serve.

This vinaigrette is good with salads containing cold meat.

Have you even eaten the base of a flower bud of an exotic thistle? You have, if you have eaten artichoke hearts, one of life's true pleasures. The raspberry vinegar in this recipe gives this vinaigrette a unique Wisconsin twist.

Nancy Lynch

Meats

One result of the dairy industry in the state was the development of a thriving meat packing industry. (The term meat packing comes from the seventeenth-century practice of packing salted pork in barrels. Refrigeration brought an end to this practice, but the name stuck.) Milwaukee and Racine were early centers of this industry, but soon it diversified geographically. Names like Hillshire Farms of New London, Patrick Cudahy of Cudahy, Jones Dairy Farm of Fort Atkinson, and Oscar Mayer & Company of Madison are recognized nationwide.

Many local butchers still make their own sausages, of which bratwurst is the most popular and well known. Some specialize in making venison sausage when processing the deer brought in by hunters. Others smoke their own bacons and hams. Nueske's, near Wausau, smokes its bacon and hams over apple wood, has a national mail-order business, and has been written up in some of the best food magazines. On the edge of Madison, the Bavaria Sausage Kitchen produces top-quality bacon, hams, and sausage. Throughout Wisconsin, in towns large and small, are some excellent neighborhood meat markets where the butcher will happily cut meat to order. Large-scale meat packing is still big business here (after all, our NFL football team pays tribute to that fact), but fortunately for us, the local butcher shop has not disappeared.

Chicken is one of the most popular meats today. Years ago it was considered expensive and was served only on Sundays. In 1941 chicken was 78 cents a pound, a lot of money in those days. On the frontier, chickens were kept for their egg-laying ability and by the time that ability was exhausted, they were generally too tough to use for anything but soup. As farmers prospered, the use of chickens for the table increased, but they were still a luxury.

From an 1844 cookbook:

Boiled chickens— Chickens should be plump, and very nicely boiled; if wanted to be particularly good, they must be boiled in a blanc. It is the fashion to send them up with tufts of cauliflower or white broccoli, divested of stems and leaves and in a white sauce.

The book also has a recipe for chicken with oysters:

Take a young fowl, fill the inside with oysters, put it into a jar, and plunge the jar in a kettle or saucepan of water. Boil it for an hour and a half. There should be a quantity of gravy from the juices of the oysters and the fowl in the jar; make it into a white sauce, with the addition of egg, cream, or a little flour and butter; add oysters to it, or serve it up plain with the fowl. The gravy that comes from a fowl dressed in this manner will be a stiff jelly the next day; the fowl will be very white and tender, and of exceeding fine flavor—advantages not obtainable in ordinary boiling—while the dish loses nothing of its delicacy or simplicity.

Visually, one can hardly imagine a less appealing dish today. It might have tasted all right, but looking at it would cause present day appetites to dwindle on the spot.

Breast of Chicken
with Artichoke Stuffing

3-4 artichoke hearts, in brine, drained
1¹/₂ cups (4 ounces) chopped mushrooms
¹/₂ leek (white part only), thoroughly cleaned
2-3 tablespoons butter
¹/₂ tablespoon minced garlic
Juice and grated rind of a lemon
Splash of half & half cream
¹/₄ cup bread crumbs
Salt and pepper to taste
4 boneless, skinless chicken breasts
¹/₂ cup white wine
1 tablespoon butter
2 tablespoons flour
¹/₄ cup half & half

. . . . .

Coarsely chop the artichoke hearts and leeks in a food processor. In a heavy sauté pan, melt the butter, add the chopped vegetables, and sauté over high heat for 3-4 minutes. Then add the garlic, cover the pan loosely, and sweat them over low heat. Add the lemon juice, cream, and bread crumbs to make a loose stuffing. Preheat oven to 350 degrees. Scoop a quarter of the stuffing onto the chicken breast, sprinkle with salt and pepper. Then carefully roll it up, putting it in a shallow roasting pan, seam-side down. Repeat with the other three breasts. Add the white wine, cover, and put in the oven.

Bake 20-30 minutes or until the breasts are tender. Remove from the pan and keep warm. Make a roux of the butter and flour and beat into the pan juices. Add grated lemon rind, and smooth mixture with cream, if necessary.

Chicken Bond

Chicken Bond honors composer Carrie Jacobs-Bond, a native of Janesville, who wrote such turn-of-the-century hits as "I Love You Truly" and "The End of a Perfect Day."

$^1/_2$ cup finely diced celery
$^1/_2$ cup finely diced carrots
$^1/_2$ cup finely diced onions
$^3/_4$ cup smoked duck, diced
2-3 tablespoons clarified butter (page 123)
$^1/_4$ cup bread crumbs
6 chicken breasts, boneless, skinless
Flour
Salt & pepper to taste
1 egg
$^1/_4$ cup water
1 cup pretzel crumbs
$^1/_4$ cup clarified butter
Gorgonzola cream sauce (page 11)

· · · · ·

Put the butter in a heavy-bottom sauté pan. Add the vegetables, cubed duck, and finally the bread crumbs. Cook on medium heat, just until vegetables soften (approximately 10 minutes).

Preheat oven to 350 degrees. Put the chicken breasts between two sheets of waxed paper and pound until meat is an even thickness. Scoop some of the filling onto a chicken breast. Fold over carefully, pound the edges slightly, and dip the stuffed chicken breast first in flour seasoned with the salt and pepper, then into the egg beaten with the water, then into the pretzel crumbs. Repeat with the remaining chicken breasts. Melt the butter in a heavy-bottom pan and brown each of the breasts on both sides in the butter. Place the pan in the oven and cook the chicken breasts through, about 20 minutes. Slice on the diagonal and serve with Gorgonzola cream sauce and wild rice (page 137). Yield: 6 servings.

Breast of Chicken
with Mushroom Stuffing

3 ounces morel or shiitake mushrooms
4 ounces white mushrooms
$^1/_2$ leek (white part), thoroughly cleaned
3-4 tablespoons butter
$^1/_2$ tablespoon garlic paste
$^1/_3$ cup half & half cream
$^1/_3$ cup freshly grated Parmesan cheese
$^1/_3$ cup bread crumbs
Salt and pepper to taste
4 chicken breasts
$^1/_2$ cup white wine

$^1/_2$ cup crumbled Gorgonzola cheese
$^1/_3$ cup half & half cream

. . . . .

Coarsely chop mushrooms and leeks separately in a food processor. In a heavy sauté pan, melt the butter and add the vegetables and sauté over high heat for 3-4 minutes till they start to give up some of their moisture. Reduce heat, add the garlic, and cover loosely to sweat until soft. Add cream, Parmesan, and bread crumbs. Preheat oven to 350 degrees. Scoop a quarter of the stuffing mixture onto one of the chicken breasts, salt and pepper it, then carefully roll it up and place, seam side down, in a shallow roasting pan. Repeat with the remaining chicken breasts. Add the wine and cover the pan.

Put the pan in the oven and bake for 20-30 minutes or until the breasts are tender. Remove the chicken breasts from the pan and keep warm. Add the crumbled Gorgonzola cheese to the pan drippings and stir to melt. Add a little cream if necessary to get the proper consistency. Arrange chicken breasts on a bed of wild rice, cover with the Gorgonzola cream, and sprinkle with a little paprika for color. Yield: 4 servings.

Chicken Primrose
or Popover Glover

*Popover Glover is
named in honor of
Joshua Glover,
whose capture and
release in 1854
prompted the
Wisconsin
Supreme Court to
challenge the
Fugitive Slave Act.*

1 pound cubed chicken, skinless & boneless
$^1/_2$ pound mushrooms, quartered
3 tablespoons clarified butter

PRIMROSE SAUCE
3 tablespoons butter
4 tablespoons flour
$1^1/_2$ cups chicken stock
1 teaspoon ground dried sage
$^1/_4$ teaspoon white pepper
$^3/_4$ cup milk, warmed
$^3/_4$ cup whipping cream, warmed
$^1/_4$ cup white wine

. . . . . .

Cook the cubed chicken and the mushrooms quickly in the clarified butter. Stir to cook evenly on all sides. Hold warm while sauce is made.

Melt the butter in a heavy-bottom sauté pan. Sprinkle in the flour and stir, cooking over low heat for a few minutes. Gradually add the chicken stock, whisking vigorously. Add the sage and white pepper. Stir in the milk and cream and continue to cook until mixture begins to thicken. Cook to a consistency you like, remove from heat, whisk in the white wine, and serve.

For Chicken Primrose, simply serve with cooked rice or wild rice. For Popover Glover, cook popovers (page 59) and split them along one side, opening out like a book. Place opened popover on the plate next to a bed of rice and spoon the chicken and sauce into the popover. Serve.

Yield: 4 servings.

Baked Chicken & Dumplings

1 roasting chicken (3-4 lbs.), quartered
Cooking oil
Freshly cracked black pepper
Salt to taste

DUMPLINGS
1 tablespoon margarine
1 egg
$^{1}/_{2}$ cup mashed potatoes
$^{1}/_{4}$ teaspoon salt
$1^{1}/_{4}$ cups flour
$^{1}/_{2}$ tablespoon baking powder
$^{1}/_{2}$ teaspoon marjoram
1 quart + 1-2 cups chicken stock

· · · · · ·

Preheat oven to 350 degrees. Sprinkle chicken with pepper and salt. In a heavy pan, brown chicken in the oil, then bake in oven for approximately 50 minutes or until internal temperature reaches 180 degrees.

While the chicken bakes, make the dumplings. Beat together the margarine, egg, and mashed potatoes until smooth. Put the chicken stock on to simmer. Add salt, flour, baking powder, and marjoram to the potato mixture. Dust your fingers with flour. Scoop up each ball of dough with a teaspoon and pat each so the shape is firm. Drop the balls into the simmering chicken stock. Simmer, turning dumplings gently until done, about 5 minutes.

Remove the chicken to a platter and keep it warm. Using the pan juices, make gravy by adding a little flour. Stir to blend and cook for a few minutes over low heat. Then add some of the chicken stock used to cook the dumplings. Serve the chicken with dumplings. Yield: 4 servings.

Dumplings appeared in many different forms on settlers' tables. They were used to fill out meals and came in everything from soup through the main dish to dessert. They were made variously from flour, raw or cooked potatoes, farina, bread, crackers, matzo meal, marrow, meat, and blood.

Beef Buchanan

Beef Buchanan honors James Buchanan, who was president when Quivey's was built and was also our only bachelor president.

4 tablespoons butter
1 (2$^1/_2$-pound center portion) beef tenderloin
2 pounds mushrooms, cleaned, trimmed, and cut up
$^1/_2$ cup finely chopped parsley
1 teaspoon crushed tarragon
$^1/_4$ cup Madeira
1 cup whipping cream
Salt and pepper to taste
1 cup minced green onions
$^1/_2$ cup freshly grated Parmesan cheese
$^1/_4$ cup bread crumbs
$^3/_4$ cup finely chopped carrots
$^3/_4$ cup finely chopped onions
$^3/_4$ cup finely chopped celery

. . . . . .

In a food processor, liquify mushrooms. Put mushrooms, parsley, tarragon, Madeira, cream, salt and pepper, and green onions into a heavy pot and cook until liquid is reduced by half. Puree the mixture in a food processor until smooth and thicken with the grated cheese and bread crumbs.

Preheat oven to 400 degrees. Cut the beef tenderloin so that it opens up into a flat piece of meat about $^1/_4$ inch thick. Spread the mushroom mixture on the meat, roll up and secure with toothpicks, then butcher's twine. Season with lemon pepper and set on the chopped vegetables. Brush the tenderloin with vegetable oil and bake for approximately 30 minutes. Let the meat stand for 15 minutes. Slice and serve with a veal demi-glace (page 19). Yield: 6 servings.

Beef Lathrop

1$^1/_2$ pounds beef tenderloin tips
1 finely chopped medium onion
$^1/_2$ teaspoon freshly grated black pepper
$^1/_2$ teaspoon basil
$^1/_2$ teaspoon thyme
2 tablespoons butter
2 tablespoons oil
3 cups beef stock reduced to 1$^1/_2$ cups

2 tablespoons margarine
2 tablespoons flour
$^3/_4$ cup sour cream
$^1/_2$ cup white wine
1 cup quartered mushrooms

* * * * *

Beef Lathrop is named for the first chancellor of the University of Wisconsin, John Lathrop. He assumed his office in 1849 when only twenty men were enrolled as students.

Cut the tenderloin tips into 2-inch chunks. Put the beef and onion in a sauté pan with the butter and oil and begin to brown. Sprinkle with the seasonings and continue cooking until all the meat is browned on all sides. Add the mushrooms, cook 5 minutes, then add the reduced stock. Simmer for 30 minutes, uncovered, or until the meat is tender.

Mix together the margarine and flour to make a roux. Add this into the simmering beef. Stir to blend. Add the sour cream, wine, and mushrooms and cook another 10 minutes.

Yield: 4-6 servings.

The Cornish pasty (rhymes with nasty, but certainly doesn't taste that way) is as regional a dish as you will find in this part of Wisconsin. Mineral Point and other small communities in the southwestern part of the state were settled in the 1820s by lead miners from Cornwall and Wales.

When the miners' wives arrived, they resumed an old tradition of baking pasties for the men to take down into the mines. The tough pastry crust could stand up to being carried in a pocket of the miner's jacket all morning. Quivey's pasties have a much more tender and flaky crust. The original also contained rutabaga with the carrots and onions—all vegetables that could readily be carried over winter in a root cellar.

Welsh miners had so little time to spare for housing, some of them lived in burrows they had dug into the hills and began to be referred to as badgers. Thus we became the "Badger State."

Mineral Point Cornish Pasty

1 recipe pie dough—your own favorite or Quivey's
   (page 163)
1 pound beef tenderloin tips or good stew meat, cubed
Cooking oil
Flour
$^1/_2$ cup chopped carrots
$^1/_2$ cup chopped onion
$^1/_2$ cup cubed potatoes
Egg beaten with a little water (egg wash)

. . . . . .

Preheat oven to 350 degrees. Roll pie dough out into four 6-inch circles.

Brown beef cubes in cooking oil. When brown on all sides, sprinkle a little flour over them and stir it in. Remove from heat.

Boil the potatoes for about 4 minutes or until they begin to get soft. Add the carrots and simmer for another 4 minutes, then add the onions and simmer for 2 more minutes. Drain and add to the meat. Mix well.

Use about $^1/_2$ cup filling for each pasty, spreading on the circle. Fold the circle over, making a semi-circular pasty. Crimp the edges with the tines of a fork. Dip the tines in flour if necessary to prevent sticking. Prick the top of each pasty with a knife to allow steam to escape. Put on a cookie sheet and place in oven. Bake about 25 minutes. When nearly done, brush tops with egg wash. Pasties should bake to golden brown. Yield: 4 pasties.

Rouladen Barstow

2 pounds good-quality pork breakfast sausage
$^1/_2$ pound Westphalian ham, diced
$1^1/_2$ cups diced mushrooms
2 cups diced onions
1 cup diced carrots
1 tablespoon crushed juniper berries
2 teaspoons caraway seeds
12 (6-ounce) beef round steaks
12 tablespoons Dusseldorf-style mustard
12 strips good-quality bacon
3 pickles, sliced into quarters lengthwise
2 ounces stuffing, approximately

ROULADEN SAUCE
6 tablespoons butter
$^3/_4$ cup flour
10 cups ($2^1/_2$ quarts) beef stock, warmed
$^1/_2$ teaspoon basil
$^1/_2$ teaspoon thyme
Black pepper to taste
$^3/_4$ cup red wine
$^1/_4$ cup tomato juice

· · · · · ·

Have your butcher cut the 12 small steaks from the round.

Prepare the sauce first and hold. Melt the butter in a large, heavy-bottom saucepan. Sprinkle in the flour and whisk, cooking for several minutes. Add in the warmed beef stock a cup at a time, continuing to whisk with each addition. Add in the herbs, pepper, red wine, and tomato juice, and simmer until needed.

Cook the sausage in a large sauté pan, breaking it apart as it cooks. Remove the sausage meat and reserve; drain off some of the fat if necessary. Add the diced ham, then the diced vegetables. Sauté until vegetables are soft. Add the juniper and caraway, and mix well. Add the sausage back into the other ingredients.

Lay out the steaks, one at a time. Each should measure about 7 x 9 inches. Spread on each one-half tablespoon of mustard, add about 2 ounces of stuffing, a pickle spear, and a strip of bacon. Fold over the sides and roll up each steak. Brown in oil in heavy Dutch oven. When all the rouladen are browned, cover with the sauce, cover the pan, and cook over medium heat until tender, about 1 hour. Remove and hold warm while sauce is cooked, on top of stove on high heat, to desired consistency.

Yield: serves 12. (If you're going to all this trouble, it might as well be for a party!) Serve with red cabbage (page 126) and spaetzle (page 40).

What can one say about pot roast except that it's an honest and hearty dish and therefore a perfect representation of Quivey's Grove? The coffee definitely adds a little kick to this pot roast.

The term "pot roast" dates back at least to 1881. It began as a convenient way to cook the tough meat from work animals. Today, tender cuts of meat are used, and pot roast remains a treasured American heritage dish.

Pot Roast

1 4-5 pound beef round, rolled and tied	STOCK
Flour	1 quart water
Salt & pepper	10 oz. beef stock
Cooking oil	1 teaspoon marjoram
1 carrot	1 teaspoon thyme
1 rib celery	1 bay leaf
1 onion, quartered	$^1/_2$ cup coffee
2 tablespoons butter	$^1/_2$ teaspoon salt
4 tablespoons flour	Freshly ground black pepper to taste

. . . . . .

Preheat the oven to 350 degrees. Dredge the beef round in flour, salt, and pepper. In a heavy-bottom kettle or pan, heat the oil. Add the beef round and brown on all sides. Then add the carrot and celery, pour the stock over the beef, and place the quartered onion on top.

Cover tightly, put in the oven, and bake until tender. This should take about 2-3 hours. When tender, remove the beef round and keep it warm. For gravy, remove the vegetables, drain, mash, and add to stock. Mix together the butter and flour to form a roux. Beat the roux into the stock.

Yield: 4-6 servings.

Quivey's serves this pot roast with small red potatoes, whole boiled onions, a carrot, and a turnip. It's equally good with mashed potatoes.

This is the lamb stew used in a popover, another of Quivey's signature dishes (page 59). The popovers can hold anything from chicken through lamb to beef and pork. You can serve this stew just as it is, or you can pop it into popovers and try your own signature dish.

Lamb Stew

2 pounds stewing lamb, cubed
Butter & cooking oil
Flour
1 teaspoon rosemary
$^1/_2$ teaspoon marjoram
2 cloves garlic, minced
3-4 carrots, peeled and chunked
1 rutabaga, peeled and cubed
4 small onions, peeled
2-3 large potatoes, peeled and cubed
$^1/_2$ cup Burgundy or other good red wine
Water

. . . . . .

In a heavy stew pan, sauté the lamb in the oil and butter. When brown on all sides, sprinkle with a little flour and the rosemary and marjoram. Stir to cover all the meat. Cook for a few minutes. Add the garlic and stir again.

Add the carrots, rutabaga, and onions, pour the wine over, and add enough water to barely cover the vegetables and meat. Cover the pan and put in the oven at 350 degrees or put on the back of the stove to simmer very gently on low heat. Add the potatoes after half an hour. Simmer until the meat and vegetables are fork-tender. Check periodically to be sure the vegetables and meat are covered with stock. The stock should thicken into gravy with cooking. Yield: 4-6 servings, depending on appetite.

Lamb Shanks Doty

Madison is the capital of Wisconsin today because of one man—James Duane Doty, attorney, explorer, and land speculator. When the U.S. government offered land for sale around the Madison lakes in 1835, Doty was one of the few early buyers, grabbing up 99 prime isthmus acres at $1.25 each. He then persuaded the legislature to make this the capital. More than a few legislators were the happy owners of choice lots in the new capital, purchased earlier from Doty for as little as ten cents each.

4 (16- 18-ounce) lamb shanks*
Flour
Salt & pepper to taste
2 tablespoons cooking oil
12 cloves garlic, peeled
2 medium onions, peeled & sliced
4 carrots, peeled & chunked
8 small new potatoes, peeled
1 cup red wine
1 sprig fresh rosemary

Preheat oven to 350 degrees. Dredge the lamb shanks in the flour seasoned with salt and pepper. Put the oil in a heavy-bottom stewing pan, add the lamb shanks, and brown on all sides over medium-high heat. Add the vegetables, turning to coat with the oil. Add the wine and rosemary, cover the pot loosely, and place in oven. Braise for about one hour, checking periodically to see that moisture is not cooking away. If it gets low, add a little water. Turn vegetables so that they brown evenly. When lamb is tender, remove with the vegetables to a warm spot. Skim off the fat and boil liquid vigorously to dissolve and reduce to 1½ cups. Serve over the shanks and vegetables. Yield: 4 servings.

* Have your butcher cut the knuckle end off the shanks for a more attractive presentation. Also, the shanks will fit in the pot more easily if they are slightly shorter.

Filet of Lamb
& Potatoes Anna
with Wild Mushrooms & Parsley Cream

GARLIC
BUTTER

*To make garlic
butter, simply take
the required
amount of butter,
melt it and add
one finely minced
or crushed clove of
garlic.*

Parsley cream sauce (recipe, page 105)
4 medium potatoes
2 tablepoons garlic butter

¹/₂ cup whipping cream
4 (5-ounce) pieces lamb loin, boned & trimmed
2 tablespoons garlic butter

. . . . .

Peel the potatoes and slice into thin rounds. Place in salted water acidulated with a little lemon juice until ready to use.

Make the parsley cream sauce.

Remove the potato slices from the water and pat dry with paper towels. Heat a tablespoon of garlic butter in each of two 8-inch non-stick pans. Place one slice of potato in the center of each pan and arrange 11 more around it, slightly overlapping each one. Put one slice in center on top, add 3 more around that. Cook, covered, over medium heat until potato is just soft, starting to brown on the bottom. The starch should hold the potato slices together, forming a cake. This will take about 5 minutes. Lift the cover again and add one tablespoon of cream to each cake, cover, and cook 2 minutes. Lift cover and add one more tablespoon of cream. Swirl pan to loosen the potato cake and allow the cream to seep underneath. Cook until cream evaporates. Hold warm. Repeat this process to make 4 cakes.

Preheat oven to 450 degrees. Heat the garlic butter in the pan and brown the filets on all sides. Bake for 8 minutes or until medium rare. Let rest in warm place.

Invert the potato cakes onto a small plate and then slide each onto the center of a serving plate. Mound the mushroom mixture in the center of the potato cake. Slice the lamb into 6 medallions and surround the potato with the medallions. Yield: serves 4.

Pork Brigham
with Apple Brandy Cream Sauce

Pork Brigham honors Colonel Ebenezer Brigham, the first permanent settler in Dane County who also became postmaster and justice of the peace.

4-pound boned and rolled
   pork loin
4 cups cider
2 teaspoons freshly grated
   black pepper
1 teaspoon garlic powder
$1/2$ teaspoon allspice
1 large onion, sliced

SAUCE
2 cups cider (reserved from
   marinade)
2 tablespoons butter
4 tablespoons flour
1 cup half & half
$1/4$ teaspoon allspice
2 tablespoons apple brandy

· · · · · ·

Mix allspice, pepper, and garlic powder into the cider. Place the pork in a glass or stainless steel container and pour cider over the meat. Cover the pan and marinate in the refrigerator overnight, turning once or twice.

Preheat the oven to 450 degrees. Transfer the pork to a roasting pan, reserving the marinade. Add $1/4$ cup of the cider marinade to the bottom of the pan and place onion slices on top of roast. Put in oven and reduce heat to 300 degrees after 15 minutes. Roast about $1^1/2$ hours (or until meat thermometer reads 170 degrees). Remove to a platter and keep warm.

For the sauce, skim fat from the roasting pan. Add 2 cups of the reserved cider to the pan and deglaze. Transfer the pan juices to a smaller pan and simmer for five minutes; strain. Set aside. In another saucepan, melt the butter over low heat, then whisk in the flour until smooth. Add half the strained pan drippings and beat with a whisk to keep smooth while continuing to cook. Whisk in remaining pan drippings. Add cream, allspice, and apple brandy. Slice the roast and serve with the sauce.

Yield: recipe should serve 4. Sauce makes 2 cups. Great with mashed potatoes, red cabbage, and applesauce.

Pork Fremont

1 large boneless pork loin, about 4 pounds
1 pound mushrooms
1 tablespoon butter
1 bunch green onions, cleaned, sliced on $1/2$-inch diagonal
1 pound kalberwurst, skinned & crumbled
$1/3$ cup apple brandy
$1/2$ teaspoon white pepper
$1/2$ pound Westphalian ham

. . . . . .

Have the butcher cut the loin so that it extends out to a rectangle.

Run the mushrooms through the large grater blade on the food processor, or coarse-chop by hand. Sauté in butter just until the mushroom juices start to come out. Put the mushrooms into a clean dish towel and squeeze out all juices, saving the juice for soup, if desired. Mix together the mushrooms, onions, kalberwurst, apple brandy, and pepper.

Spread out the pork. Layer the ham on the pork. Spread the stuffing on the ham, about $1/4$-inch deep. Roll the pork roast up and tie with string. Season with pepper. Serve with an apple brandy cream sauce (page 98). Yield: 6 servings.

Pork Fremont honors John Fremont, who was the Republican candidate for president in 1856, the year after Quivey's was built. Fremont carried Wisconsin, but the Democrat, John Buchanan, won the election.

Schurz Schnitzle

Schurz Schnitzle honors the intellectual German refugee Carl Schurz, who emigrated to Wisconsin after the unsuccessful German revolution of 1848. Schurz became a strong advocate against slavery and served the Union in the Civil War. His wife established America's first kindergarten, in Watertown.

4 (2-ounce) slices from cidered pork loin*
Flour
1 egg beaten with a little water
1 cup pretzel crumbs
3-4 tablespoons clarified butter

. . . . . .

Pound the slices of pork till thin. Start to heat the clarified butter in the pan. Dip the pork slices in the flour, then in the egg, then pretzel crumbs. Drop in the hot butter and sauté quickly on each side (about 1^1/$_2$ minutes). Put on a plate and serve with twice-baked potatoes and sautéed apples. Pour any pan juices over the meat. Serve. Yield: 2 servings.

*See recipe for Pork Brigham, page 98.

In the early days of Wisconsin, when most farms raised pigs, at least one was slaughtered each fall to provide meat for the winter. The fresh meat was eaten first, of course, and since the season also produced an abundance of apples, a natural partnership developed between pork and apples. Quivey's has a stuffed pork chop that is a succulent, tender reminder of the joys of this good partnership. This is a recipe for two. You may double it for four.

This recipe is a good example of the difficulties of restaurant cooking. The recipe was developed, tested, and found to be delicious. However, there was no way to offer it on the menu successfully. If held, the pork chops dried out; if cooked to order, they took too long to prepare. So the recipe went into the Quivey's Grove file, only to be offered now for home cooks.

Stuffed Pork Chops

2 pork chops, with pockets
1 tablespoon butter
1 small apple, peeled, cored, and diced fine
$^{1}/_{4}$ cup finely chopped onion
$^{1}/_{4}$ cup finely chopped celery
$^{1}/_{4}$ cup finely chopped fresh mushrooms
1 slice rye bread, crust removed
Fresh bread crumbs
$^{1}/_{4}$ teaspoon crumbled sage
Pinch salt
Freshly ground black pepper to taste
Generous pinch ground cloves
$^{1}/_{2}$ cup fresh cider

. . . . . .

Have your butcher prepare two double chops with a pocket cut for the stuffing.

Preheat oven to 350 degrees. In a sauté pan, melt the butter, add the apple, onion, celery, and mushroom. Stir gently to mix and cover to sweat the fruit and vegetables. When the

A PIG ROAST
PICNIC

*Assorted
Wisconsin cheeses
and crackers*

*Whole smoke-
roasted pig*

*Apple butter
barbecue sauce*

*Barbecued black
beans*

*Corn and jalapeno
muffins*

Parmesan potatoes

Sourdough bread

Cole slaw

Apple crisp

onions have become translucent, remove pan from the burner and add the rye bread, torn in small pieces. Mix. If mixture is wet, add a few bread crumbs. If too dry, add a little cider.

Force stuffing into pockets in chops. In a sauté pan, quickly sear the chops in a little oil. When they are brown on both sides, remove from the burner and drain off excess oil. Pour the cider over the chops, cover the pan, and put in the oven. Bake for about 45 minutes or until the pork is tender. Because of the stuffing, the chops will take longer than usual.

At Quivey's the chops are served with a twice-baked potato and homemade applesauce. They are also delicious with Squash Timbales (page 134). Yield: 2 servings.

Veal Harvey
or Veal in Caper & Mustard Sauce

4 (5- 6-ounce) veal filets
Freshly ground black pepper
Flour
Cooking oil
3 tablespoons olive oil
1 leek, white only, thinly sliced & thoroughly cleaned
3 tablespoons capers
1 tablespoon green peppercorns
$^1/_4$ cup white wine
2 teaspoons Dijon-style mustard
$^1/_2$ cup chicken stock
1 tablespoon lemon zest

· · · · ·

Dredge the veal filets in the pepper and flour. Brown in oil until meat is medium rare. Remove and keep warm. Add the olive oil and the leeks. Stir. Cook for 5 minutes. Add the capers, peppercorns, white wine, and mustard. Stir to blend well, and continue simmering. Add the chicken stock and lemon zest. Simmer just until leeks are fork-tender.

Pour the sauce over the veal, garnish with extra lemon zest, and serve. Yield: 4 servings.

Veal Harvey honors Cordelia Harvey, wife of Louis P. Harvey, Governor of Wisconsin. Governor Harvey drowned 73 days after his inauguration in January, 1862, while taking medical supplies to Wisconsin soldiers wounded in the battle of Shiloh. His wife, Cordelia, took up his work with wounded soldiers and became known as "the Wisconsin angel." She persuaded President Lincoln to establish a series of soldiers' hospitals in the North, including three in Wisconsin at Milwaukee, Madison, and Prairie du Chien.

Veal Chops
with Horseradish Apple Cream

*Veal is an
important
Wisconsin
commodity, one
of the many by-
products of the
dairy industry.
Each year
thousands of calves
are born, many of
them male. Only a
very few of these
are needed for the
propagation of the
dairy herds; the
rest are destined to
become veal for
our tables.
Wisconsin veal is
known throughout
the country as
some of the best
obtainable. It has
appeared on
Wisconsin tables
since the dairy
industry began.*

$^1/_2$ cup cider
$^2/_3$ cup heavy cream
1 tablespoon apple butter
2 teaspoons fresh horseradish*
1-2 tablespoons apple brandy
$^1/_2$ cup crème fraîche (page 40)
4 veal chops
2 tablespoons butter
3 tablespoons cooking oil

· · · · · ·

Put the cider and heavy cream in a small, heavy-bottom pot, and boil to reduce by a third. Remove from the heat and add in the apple butter and horseradish. Add the apple brandy, stirring to blend well. When mixture has cooled slightly, add in the crème fraîche and beat well to incorporate. Hold warm.

Preheat oven to 425. Over high heat, quickly sear the chops in the butter and oil. Cover the chops and put in the oven and bake till chops are medium rare. (Time will depend on thickness of the chops.) Remove and put chops on plates. Pour sauce over chops. Good with wild rice or with mashed potatoes. Yield: 4 servings.

*Horseradish loses its pungency quickly. To be sure you have the right stuff, purchase it as needed and read the label carefully. Do not use horseradish cut with turnips, since it will be too mild for this recipe.

Sautéed Veal & Smoked Pork
with Parsley Cream on Potato Cakes & Fresh Asparagus

24 stems medium asparagus

PARSLEY CREAM SAUCE
10-15 stems parsley
1 cup finely diced wild mushrooms
$^1/_2$ cup finely diced leek, white section only
2 tablespoons clarified butter
1 clove garlic, minced
2 cups whipping cream
2 tablespoons Madeira
Salt & pepper to taste

POTATO CAKES
$^1/_2$ cup diced onion
3 tablespoons butter
$^3/_4$ cup half & half cream
1 teaspoon salt
$^1/_2$ teaspoon black pepper
2 cups shredded potatoes
$^1/_4$ cup freshly grated Parmesan cheese
2 eggs
1 cup bread crumbs
3 tablespoons clarified butter

VEAL
12 ounces veal round
4 ounces smoked pork loin
2 tablespoons clarified butter
4 large shiitake mushroom caps, sliced
$^1/_4$ cup julienned leek (white part only)
$^1/_4$ cup asparagus stems, sliced
4 cloves garlic
$^1/_4$ teaspoon salt

. . . . . .

Wash the asparagus and cut off the tough, fibrous ends. Steam over boiling water approximately 4 minutes until cooked but still crunchy. Plunge into cold water to stop cooking. Trim spears to uniform 4-inch length. Slice trimmings into rounds and reserve to go with veal.

For the parsley cream sauce, remove stems from the parsley and blanch in a small amount of boiling water for three minutes. Drain and cool. Squeeze out all water. Sauté the mushrooms and leek in butter on high heat until soft. Add the garlic, lower the heat, and cook one minute. Add half the cream, raise the heat, and boil vigorously till very thick. Add remainder of cream and boil till it coats a spoon thickly. Add the parsley and warm for about 2 minutes, breaking up the parsley. Add the Madeira and salt and pepper to taste. Hold warm.

For the potato cakes, sauté the onions in butter for 3-4 minutes, add salt, pepper, and cream. Bring to a boil, add the potatoes and reduce heat. Cook, stirring occasionally, until the cream thickens with the potato starch. Add Parmesan cheese and allow the mixture to cool. Add the eggs and mix well. Form into 4 equal cakes about $1/2$-inch thick. Coat with bread crumbs. Sauté in a hot pan in butter until brown on one side. Turn and lower heat to cook through. Hold in a warm oven while preparing the veal.

Slice the veal and pork into $1/4$-inch strips. Slice mushroom caps into strips. Smash the garlic with salt and reserve. Sauté the veal in the butter in a hot pan for 3 minutes. Add the pork, garlic, mushrooms, leeks, and asparagus and sauté another 2 minutes. Add half the parsley cream to the pan and stir to coat. Heat through and reserve.

Coat each of 4 plates with the parsley cream. Place warm asparagus spears like the spokes of a wheel on the cream. Top with a potato cake. Top potato cake with veal mixture and garnish with fresh parsley. Yield: 4 servings.

Veal Vilas

2 large veal chops
Butter
$^1/_2$ cup sliced wild mushrooms
$^1/_2$ cup diagonally sliced green onions
$^1/_2$ cup port wine
$^1/_2$ cup demi-glace (page 19)
$^1/_2$ cup heavy cream
$1^1/_2$ tablespoons chopped fresh thyme
2 stuffed tomatoes
4 boiled red potatoes

. . . . . .

Preheat oven to 425 degrees. Brown the chops in butter, then add the mushrooms and green onions. Sauté for 3 minutes, then add the wine. Cover and put in hot oven, and bake until the chops are medium rare. Remove pan from oven, remove chops from pan, and keep them warm. Add the demi-glace, cream, and fresh thyme and cook gently on top of the stove, on high heat, stirring constantly to reduce. When sauce has begun to thicken, put the chops on a plate, drizzle a little sauce over the chops, and serve. Yield: 2 servings.

Veal Vilas honors the mayor of Madison, L. B. Vilas, who stated in his 1861 inaugural: "People have been swindled so often and so much by those elected . . . it's not surprising that some look at government as a means by which the few can rob the many." Amen.

Osso Bucco is a traditional Italian dish. Between 1905 and 1910 a large number of Italians immigrated to Madison, from southern Italy and Sicily. This population settled in a section of town called Greenbush, an eighty-acre parcel bounded by Mills, Regent, Murray, and Erin streets.

Osso Bucco

8 veal shanks
Flour
Cooking oil
1½ cups finely diced onions
1½ cups finely diced celery
1½ cups finely diced carrots
4-5 tablespoons butter
2-3 cloves garlic, minced
Zest of ½ lemon
1 cup white wine

1 cup beef consomme
1½ cups diced tomatoes, with juice, peeled and seeded
1 teaspoon dried basil
Freshly ground black pepper to taste
½ teaspoon dried thyme
2 bay leaves

. . . . . .

Dredge the veal shanks in flour and brown on all sides in the oil. Reserve.

Sauté the onions, celery, and carrots in butter. Add the garlic and strips of lemon peel to the mixture and spread it out in the bottom of a roasting pan. Put the veal shanks on the vegetables in roasting pan. Pour off the fat from the veal pan and deglaze the pan with the white wine and pour over the contents of the roasting pan, then pour consomme over all.

Preheat oven to 350 degrees. Mix the diced tomatoes with the herbs and the pepper and spread this in the pan as well. Bake for 2-2½ hours or until the veal is perfectly tender. Remove shanks and keep warm. Reduce the vegetable stock if desired. Serve the shanks with the vegetables on a bed of rice or noodles. Yield: 6-8 servings.

The Mugwump

A mugwump was a Republican who refused to support the party's candidate, James G. Blaine, in the campaign of 1884. Since then it has come to mean someone who cannot decide, who sits with his mug on one side of the fence and his wump on the other. At Quivey's, it is the name of an entree of both Beef Buchanan and Pork Fremont, for someone who cannot decide which to order.

Nancy Lynch

Fish & Game

Wisconsin has always been abundant in fish and game. The departing glacier blessed the region with lakes, streams, and rivers, all teeming with fish. Cisco, lake chubs, whitefish, smelt, perch, muskellunge, pike, bass, trout, sturgeon, crappies, blue gills, catfish, and bullheads have sustained Wisconsin inhabitants for countless generations.

The Friday night fish fry is quintessential Wisconsin fare. It can be found in the smallest hamlet in the state as well as in Milwaukee and Madison. The fish ranges from walleye filets to lake perch and often includes ocean species, especially cod and ocean perch, obviously not native to the state.

Game was also plentiful: elk, moose, woodland caribou, bison, white-tailed deer, grouse, quail, wild turkey, and migrating wild ducks and Canada geese all added to the food supply of Wisconsin's early settlers. In addition, those hardy pioneers enjoyed feasting on bear, beaver, raccoon, and other meats that most of us now consider inappropriate for the table. They had fewer options than we do today, of course. They ate what they could catch or shoot or trap while they cleared land and prepared to begin farming.

The hunting and fishing tradition has remained strong in Wisconsin since those early days. Dining on fish and game is a tradition here. Quivey's honors those early settlers with some of its own recipes for Wisconsin's bounty.

Catfish
with Corn & Cucumber Relish

RELISH
2 ears of corn, blanched
1 cucumber, peeled, seeded and diced
1 red pepper, cored, seeded and diced
1 large red onion, peeled and diced
2 jalapeno peppers, cored and diced*
2 tomatoes, cored, seeded and diced
1$^1/_2$ tablespoons fresh ginger, peeled and diced
3 cloves garlic, peeled and diced
1 bunch cilantro
Juice of 1 grapefruit
Juice of 2 limes
Juice of 2 lemons
2 tablespoons olive oil
1 tablespoon salt

1-1$^1/_2$ pounds catfish filets
Flour
Butter

. . . . .

For the relish, remove the corn kernels from the cobs and put into a large bowl. Add the cucumber, red pepper, onion, jalapenos, tomato, ginger, garlic, and cilantro, and stir to blend well. Beat together the citrus juices, olive oil, and salt. Pour over vegetables, stir to blend well, and refrigerate until needed.

When you are ready to cook the catfish, remove the bowl of relish from the refrigerator and allow it to come to room temperature. Dust the catfish filets in flour. Heat the butter in a sauté pan. Add the filets and cook quickly over high heat. Turn the filets out on serving plates, top with relish, and serve. Extra relish may be served separately. Yield: 4 servings.

* If you have sensitive skin, wear rubber gloves while working with jalapeno peppers.

Cod was one of the mainstays of the early New England fishing industry. It's a lean, firm-fleshed, mild white fish that adapts readily to a variety of cooking methods and is a feature of cuisines as diverse as Norwegian, Scottish, and French. Dried or smoked, it will last a long time. Haddock, hake, and pollock are all members of the cod family.

Baked Cod with Herb Butter

HERB BUTTER
$^1/_2$ pound butter
$2^1/_2$ teaspoons fresh rosemary, chopped
$^1/_2$ teaspoon fresh dill, chopped
$2^1/_2$ teaspoons fresh thyme, chopped
Pinch of salt
1 clove garlic, put through garlic press
Juice of $^1/_2$ lemon
Grated zest of 1 lemon (yellow part only)

1-1$^1/_2$ pounds cod filets
Paprika

· · · · · ·

Put all the ingredients for the herb butter into a pan. Mix and heat until the butter is melted.

Preheat oven to 350 degrees. Put the cod filets in a shallow baking pan, and lightly drizzle some of the herb butter onto the fish. Sprinkle the fish with paprika, put in the oven, and bake for 20 minutes. Fish should flake easily when tested with a fork. Drizzle remaining herb butter over fish before serving. Yield: 4 servings.

There are still numerous trout to be caught in Wisconsin's streams and rivers. However, there are also many farms now raising trout, on demand and throughout the year, for restaurant and home use. From whichever source it comes to your table, fresh rainbow trout, properly cooked, is a delicacy to be savored.

Baked Rainbow Trout
with Dill, Green Onion, & Mustard Butter

$^1/_4$ teaspoon dill weed
3 tablespoons chopped green onion
3 tablespoons butter, softened
1 tablespoon chopped fresh parsley
2 tablespoons lemon juice
$^1/_2$ teaspoon Dijon-style mustard
$^1/_8$ teaspoon garlic powder
1 (1-pound) rainbow trout

· · · · · ·

Mix all ingredients, except the trout, together, being sure to blend well.

Place the trout in a shallow pan. Preheat oven to 325 degrees. Put about three-quarters of the butter into the trout's cavity, then spread the rest on top. Place the trout in the oven and bake for about 20-25 minutes. The fish should flake easily when tested with a fork. Watch carefully, as fish dries out quickly when overcooked. Serve at once with wild rice and a light, dry white wine. Yield: Serves two, or one very generously.

Lake Trout
in Horseradish Crust

2$^1/_2$ cups seasoned croutons
3 tablespoons prepared horseradish, squeezed dry
4 ounces smoked trout
4 ounces grated fresh Parmesan cheese
4 ounces butter, chunked
1-1$^1/_2$ pounds boneless, skinless lake trout filets
2 tablespoons butter
2 tablespoons cooking oil

Process the croutons with the horseradish, smoked trout, cheese, and butter until it resembles coarse meal. Set aside. Preheat the oven to 350 degrees.

Sear the filets quickly in the butter and oil. Top with the horseradish topping and bake in the oven until done, about 12 minutes. Test with a fork; the fish should flake easily. Serve over fresh tomato coulis (page 144) with boiled vegetables. Yield: 4 servings.

Salmon with Ginger & Lime

Although salmon have been introduced into the Great Lakes for sport fishing, most of the salmon you purchase is farm-raised, just as catfish and mussels are. Fish farming helps to stabilize the supply of fish, assures its quality, protects a valuable natural resource, and aids the state's economy.

$^1/_2$ tablespoon peeled & grated fresh ginger
Juice and zest of 1 lime (green part only)
2 (8-10 ounce) salmon filets
$^1/_4$ cup canola oil
Salt & white pepper to taste
1 whole garlic clove
$^1/_4$ medium onion, sliced
$^1/_2$ cup Sauvignon Blanc wine
1 green onion, sliced thin
4 tablespoons butter
$^1/_2$ cup whipping cream
1 tablespoon chopped fresh parsley

Peel and grate the ginger. Reserve. Grate lime peel, taking only the green part. Cut lime in half and squeeze out juice. Reserve.

Skin the filets and remove the belly fat, if any. Reserve the trimmings. Make a marinade of the lime juice, oil, salt, and pepper. Marinate the filets overnight.

Put the salmon trimmings in a pan, cover them with water, and add the wine, garlic, and onion. Simmer for 15 minutes, then strain and reduce to $^1/_2$ cup.

Sauté the scallions in half the butter until soft. Add the reduced stock and the cream and reduce by half. Beat in the remaining butter bit by bit. Reduce the heat to medium-low. Add the lime juice, parsley, and ginger and keep the mixture warm. Preheat oven to 350 degrees.

Put the salmon in a shallow roasting pan and bake for 15-20 minutes till fish flakes easily when tested with a fork. Remove immediately to warm plates, drizzle a little sauce over the salmon, garnish with the lime zest, and serve with tomato coulis (page 144). Yield: serves 2.

The Friday night fish fry is quintessential Wisconsin fare. It can be found in the smallest hamlet as well as in Milwaukee and Madison. The fish ranges from walleye filets to perch and often includes ocean species, especially cod and perch— obviously not native to the state.

Potter Perch

1 bottle of beer or cup of buttermilk
1 cup flour
1 tablespoon seasoning salt
1 teaspoon freshly cracked pepper

WITH PRETZEL CRUMBS AND CORNMEAL
1 egg
$^1/_4$ cup water, beaten with egg
$^1/_2$ cup cornmeal
$^1/_2$ cup pretzel crumbs

1-1$^1/_2$ pounds fresh perch (or other) filets

. . . . . .

Begin to preheat the oil so that it reaches 375 degrees by the time the filets are ready.

For each coating, mix the seasonings with the flour. Dip the filets in the wetting agent (beer, buttermilk, or egg wash), then in the seasoned flour or cornmeal and pretzel crumbs. Drop each filet carefully into the hot fat and fry until brown and crispy on all sides. This takes 5-7 minutes depending on the thickness of the filets. Drain on paper towels and serve immediately, accompanied by a good local beer, coleslaw, and french-fried potatoes (cooked separately from the fish!). Yield: 4-6 servings.

Potter Perch honors the Wisconsin congressman who, while debating abolition, was challenged to a duel by Rep. Pryor of Virginia. When Pryor named bowie knives as his weapons of choice, Potter indignantly withdrew, declaring he was no butcher.

Walleye Smith

1¹/₄ pounds walleye filets
Crème fraîche (page 40)
Fresh dill weed

. . . . . .

Preheat oven to 425 degrees. Place the walleye in a shallow
ovenproof dish. Spread the crème fraîche over the filets and
sprinkle with chopped fresh dill weed. Bake in the oven,
watching carefully to be sure the fish does not overcook. The
fish should flake easily when touched with a fork but should
not be dry or rubbery. Serve with baked potatoes. Yield: 4
servings.

Hasenpfeffer

1 rabbit, quartered
2 strips good bacon, cooked

MARINADE
1 cup water
1 cup red wine
1 cup chopped onion
1 tablespoon pickling spices
$^1/_2$ teaspoon salt

Freshly ground black
   pepper to taste
1 teaspoon thyme
1-2 bay leaves, depending
   on size

SAUCE
2 tablespoons red wine or
   balsamic vinegar
2 tablespoons honey
1 tablespoon butter
2 tablespoons flour

· · · · · ·

Wash the rabbit and pat dry with paper towels. Put in a glass, stainless steel, or other non-reactive bowl.

Put the water and red wine in a stainless steel or other non-reactive saucepan and bring to a boil. Add in all the other marinade ingredients. Pour over the rabbit, cool, and cover. Marinate overnight.

Preheat oven to 350 degrees. Remove the rabbit from the marinade and put in a roasting pan. Bring the marinade to a boil and pour over the rabbit. Sprinkle cooked, crumbled bacon on top of rabbit. Cover the pan and place in the oven. Cook for about an hour or until the rabbit is tender.

Remove the rabbit from the pan to a warm place. Strain the marinade and bring to a boil. Remove from the heat, then add the honey and vinegar. Mix the butter and flour together to make a thick paste and thicken the sauce with it, beating well to incorporate. Serve the rabbit with the sauce. Yield: 2-4 servings.

"To make a rabbit taste much like a hare, choose one that is young but full-grown, hang it in the skin three or four days; then skin it; and lay it, without washing, in a seasoning of black pepper, and allspice in a very powder, a glass of portwine, and the same quantity of vinegar. Baste it occasionally for forty hours; then stuff it, and roast it as a hare, and with the same sauce. Do not wash off the liquor it was soaked in."

—*From* A New System of Domestic Cookery, *by Mrs. Rundell of Philadelphia. Used by Betsey Wade, Wade House Stagecoach Inn, Greenbush, Wisconsin*

Here is another delicious and easy way to cook rabbit, which is a savory alternative to baked or fried chicken. Rabbit has a mild flavor, an excellent texture, and is rich in protein. The pretzels in this recipe, seasoned with allspice and nutmeg, make a delicious coating.

Baked Rabbit in Cider

1 rabbit (2-2^1/$_2$ pounds), cut up
1 egg
^{1}/$_4$ cup water
1^1/$_4$ cups pretzel crumbs
^{1}/$_2$ teaspoon allspice
^{1}/$_2$ teaspoon nutmeg
4 ounces melted butter or margarine
1 cup cider

. . . . . .

Preheat the oven to 350 degrees. Wash rabbit and pat dry with paper towels. Beat the egg and the water together. Put the pretzel crumbs in a bag with the spices, and shake to mix. Dip the pieces of rabbit in the egg wash, then shake each piece gently in the bag of seasoned crumbs till completely coated. Lay each piece in a shallow baking dish. When all the rabbit has been coated, pour the melted margarine or butter over the pieces and then put the dish in the oven. Bake for ^{1}/$_2$ hour, then pour cider over the rabbit. Bake another ^{1}/$_2$ hour or until the rabbit appears done. The meat will be firm, but should cut easily. Yield: 2-4 servings.

Since rabbit is the leanest of meats, you can indulge and serve it with broccoli hollandaise or another rich vegetable dish. It's also excellent with a winter salad of spinach, citrus fruit, and toasted walnuts.

If desired, when you remove the rabbit from the pan, add a little more cider to the pan and loosen all the bits as you stir. Simmer for a few moments, then pour over the rabbit.

Buffalo meat is much lower in cholesterol and saturated fat than beef. Buffalo raising also has ecological advantages, since three buffalo will grow to market weight on the same amount of pasture it takes to raise two beef cattle, while raising about one third to one half more meat than the cattle.

Buffalo Stew

$^1/_2$ pound good, smoky bacon, diced
2 pounds buffalo chuck, cut in 2-inch cubes
Flour
1 teaspoon paprika
1 large onion, peeled & chopped
2 cups dark beer
$^1/_2$ cup coffee
1 pound uncooked pork or game sausage, sliced
1-2 tablespoons strong seeds and berries—black mustard, pepper, cumin, caraway, fennel, and juniper to taste

. . . . . .

Preheat oven to 350 degrees. Cook bacon and sausage in heavy pan. Remove, drain, and reserve. Dredge buffalo cubes in flour and brown them well in the fat. Remove and reserve. Add the paprika and the onions and sauté until the onions are soft. Add the beer and coffee to deglaze the pan. Add the meats back to the pan. Add the seasonings. This stew is meant to be fairly robust in flavor.

Lightly cover the pan and place in the oven. Check and adjust the moisture. Meats should brown and not be completely covered with the sauce. The sauce should thicken to gravy as it cooks, about $1^1/_2$ hours.

The stew should be served with boiled potatoes, carrots, turnips, or rutabagas. These can be cooked separately and added at the end, or parboiled and added to the meats about an hour after the meat has begun to cook. Or the meat may be served with noodles or spaetzle. Yield: 4-6 servings.

Wisconsin is as far east as buffalo were found when the European immigrants began their westward expansion. Because the animal was so useful, giving meat, fur, and hide for leather, it was quickly hunted to extinction here as it nearly was elsewhere. In 1982 there were three men in Wisconsin raising buffalo, with most of the calves going to other game farms and zoos around the world. By 1992 there were 70 people raising buffalo in Wisconsin, most of them for meat.

Venison is popular in Wisconsin, which has one of the largest white-tailed deer populations in the country. In 1991, Wisconsin hunters killed a record 352,520 during the season. Venison, which is available in some specialty meat markets, is a mild red meat that takes well to seasoning. It is a lean meat, with good flavor. Here is one of Quivey's favorite venison recipes..

Venison Tenderloin
with Roasted Shallots and Garlic

4-6 shallots, peeled
4-6 cloves garlic, peeled
2 tablespoons clarified butter (see facing page)
1 cup shiitake mushrooms, de-stemmed & sliced
1 cup red Burgundy wine
1 cup demi-glace (page 19)
2 teaspoons fresh rosemary
$^1/_2$ tablespoon juniper berries, crushed
2 tablespoons clarified butter
$^1/_2$ cup flour, seasoned with salt & pepper
$1^1/_2$-2 pounds venison tenderloin, trimmed & cleaned of
    silverskin

· · · · · ·

Preheat oven to 350 degrees. Sauté the shallots and garlic in the butter to coat, then put them in a pan in the oven and roast until soft and browned. Remove from the oven and add the sliced mushrooms. Sauté over medium heat until soft. Add the wine and reduce till almost dry. Add demi-glace, rosemary, juniper and heat for 5 minutes. Adjust seasonings with salt and pepper. Hold warm.

Dredge the tenderloin in seasoned flour and brown it in the clarified butter. Roast the tenderloin until medium rare, about 10 minutes. Remove and let rest 10 minutes. Slice into medallions $^1/_4$-inch thick. Pool the sauce on service plates and fan the venison over. Yield: 4 servings.

Serve this with rosemary mashed potatoes and braised red cabbage, with wild rice and winter squash.

* To clarify $\frac{1}{2}$-pound of butter, melt it over low heat in a heavy-bottom pan. Skim off the foam from the top. Pour off the fat, leaving the milky residue at the bottom of the pan. The clear fat is clarified butter. Use what you need and refrigerate the rest for later use. Clarified butter, also called drawn butter, has a higher burning point than ordinary butter, but less flavor.

Nancy Lynch

Vegetables & Sauces

Wisconsin is, of course, the dairy state. But its agricultural bounty does not end there. Wisconsin produces nearly one half of all the nation's cranberries. It is one of the major mint producers, ranking just behind Oregon. We rank third in the production of maple syrup, even though less than five percent of our available trees are tapped.

Wisconsin agriculture really shines, however, when it comes to vegetables. The state ranks number one in the nation in the production of canned vegetables.

In 1883 Albert Landreth began experimenting with canning peas in Wisconsin. In 1887 he built a canning plant and by 1889 the state stood third nationally in the production of canned peas. By the turn of the century there were twenty-one vegetable canneries in operation. Plants in Cassville, Randolph, Platteville, Sauk City, Kewaunee, and Burlington were canning tomatoes, corn, peas, sauerkraut, and pickles. The last year of World War II, 1945, was the zenith year for canning vegetables in Wisconsin. After the war, freezing made serious inroads into the vegetable canning industry, and now Wisconsin is a leader in both canning and freezing.

Vegetables statistics in Wisconsin remain impressive. The state ranks fifth in the nation in potato production. It is fourth in carrots, third in pickling cucumbers, second in beet production, and first in sweet peas, sweet corn, and snap beans. In a good year, Wisconsin produces more than a hundred thousand tons of sauerkraut, enough for a lifetime of bratwurst sandwiches at Milwaukee Brewers home baseball games.

One of the most popular vegetable dishes at Quivey's Grove is braised red cabbage, a traditional German dish. An old recipe uses currant jelly in place of the brown sugar called for here, and recommends boiling the cabbage for 2 hours! It also uses a bay leaf. The currant jelly and the bay leaf might be worth a try. Boiling cabbage for two hours is definitely not.

Braised Red Cabbage

2 slices good bacon
1 cup cider vinegar
1 cup water
1^{1}/$_{3}$ cups brown sugar
1 head cabbage, sliced fine
2 apples, cored & diced
1 onion, sliced
Salt to taste
^{1}/$_{2}$ teaspoon black pepper

· · · · ·

Cook the strips of bacon in a large pan. Remove the bacon and reserve for another use. Add the vinegar, water, and brown sugar to the bacon grease. Blend well and heat through. Add the cabbage, apples, onion, salt, and pepper. Cook for 20 minutes, stirring occasionally. Do not overcook as the cabbage will lose all its color. Yield: 4-6 servings.

According to The Chef's Companion, *the leek is Mediterranean in origin, so it may have been brought to the British Isles by the Romans. (Emperor Nero is said to have been especially fond of them.) "An ancient member of the lily family . . . more subtle flavor than that of other onions . . . because it lacks a well defined bulb dirt gets down into its leaves, necessitating careful washing."*

The leek, national symbol of Wales, is associated with the patron saint David, who served as bishop there until 610 A.D. and who ordered his troops to wear leeks into battle against the Saxons. Later, when the Welsh resisted English domination, they went off to war with a leek pinned to their caps as a sign of St. David's protection and approval. Unfortunately the leek didn't do the trick this time, and Wales is now part of Great Britain.

Many of southwestern Wisconsin's early lead miners came here from Wales and had a better use for the sturdy vegetable than as a badge in battle. The leek thus became part of Wisconsin's vegetable heritage and is now honored by its use in many of Quivey's dishes.

Leeks grow especially well in Wisconsin. The first of the leek harvest begins to appear at the farmers' markets starting around the end of August, and the harvest lasts right through Thanksgiving.

Crispy Leek Ribbons

2 leeks
1 cup flour

Salt & pepper to taste
Oil for frying

. . . . . .

Heat the oil to 375 degrees in a deep pan. Clean the leeks by cutting off the root end and the green tops. Split the leeks lengthwise. Wash the dirt out, gently separating the layers. Shake dry. Cut lengthwise into 1/4-inch ribbons. Season the flour with salt and pepper, and dredge the ribbons in the flour. Fry the leeks till they are golden brown and crisp, then drain them on paper towels. They are beautiful and tasty with steaks or lamb. Yield: enough ribbons for 4 servings.

This recipe is a variation on tradition. It's a savory bread pudding, rather than a sweet. It uses garlic and green onions and makes a fine companion to steaks and chops. It also makes a fancy accompaniment to prime rib, in place of the usual Yorkshire pudding.

Green Onion and Garlic Bread Pudding

1 cup whipping cream
1 egg
1 egg yolk
$1/4$ teaspoon salt
1 tablespoon crushed fresh garlic
3 green onions, finely sliced
2 cups sourdough bread cubes, $1/2$-inch

· · · · · ·

Combine the cream, eggs, salt, and half of the onions. Let sit in the refrigerator for 2 hours. Preheat oven to 350 degrees. Grease well six 4-ounce custard cups. Divide the bread cubes evenly among the six cups and pour the egg mixture over the bread. Put the remaining onions on top, pushing down slightly, if necessary. Put the custard cups in a shallow pan and put the pan in the oven. Bake for 35 minutes or until the custard sets and the puddings are brown on top.

Yield: 6 servings.

Mashed potatoes are a major comfort food for pretty nearly everyone. Memories of them accompanying grandmother's southern fried chicken, or a superlative meat loaf, or a roast of some kind are ones many of us carry with us. Quivey's has taken that memory and added a little kick. It makes us feel more grown-up when eating them. But these mashed potatoes still have the power to comfort and soothe.

Garlic Mashed Potatoes

3 pounds potatoes, peeled
2 tablespoons fresh garlic, peeled
$^1/_2$ cup freshly grated Parmesan cheese
$^1/_2$ cup sour half-and-half
4 ounces butter, softened
3 green onions, trimmed and chopped
Salt & white pepper to taste

. . . . . .

Boil potatoes until very tender. Combine garlic, cheese, sour cream, butter, and green onions in the bowl of a food processor. Process until combined. Drain the potatoes and put in a large bowl. Add the processed mixture and cream the potatoes, using an electric mixer or by hand, until the potatoes are smooth. Season with salt and pepper and serve.

Yield: 4-6 servings.

Here's another potato recipe that sparks up plain boiled new potatoes with fresh life, making them elegant enough for a dinner party.

Smashed Potatoes

$^1/_3$ cup combined chopped fresh basil, rosemary, parsley & chives
$^1/_3$ cup butter, melted
1 cup whipping cream
3 cloves garlic, peeled
2-2$^1/_2$ pounds new red potatoes

. . . . .

When combining the herbs, remove rosemary leaves from tough woody stems and remove parsley from stems. Add all the herbs to the melted butter and mix well. Hold warm.

Simmer the garlic in the cream till the garlic is very soft. Strain and puree the garlic and add back to the cream. Add this garlic cream to the melted herb butter mixture and blend. Hold warm.

Boil the new potatoes until fork tender and skins begin to split. Drain and smash with a potato masher. Add the melted herb butter to the potatoes and serve.

Yield: 4-6 servings.

In 1840 potatoes topped Wisconsin's list of cash crops with just under a half-million bushels; ten years later the state produced a million and a half. By 1880 Wisconsin ranked second in production with 13.5 million bushels. The state now ranks fifth among major potato producers but is still first in the Midwest. One acre of Wisconsin potatoes could sustain a family of four for a hundred years.

The final potato recipe is for twice-baked potatoes, which rank right up there as a memorable childhood comfort food. This recipe will serve four and can accompany just about anything. Because the potatoes are so rich, a lean meat is a good partner. And, because they incorporate cheese and egg yolk, these potatoes can even serve as a main course, accompanied only by a tossed green salad.

Twice Baked Potatoes

4 russet or baking potatoes
1 egg yolk
$1/3$ cup grated Cheddar cheese
2 ounces cream cheese, softened
$1/4$ teaspoon white pepper
$1/2$ teaspoon salt
$1/2$ teaspoon onion salt
$1/2$ teaspoon garlic salt
4-5 tablespoons butter
$1/2$ cup cream

. . . . . .

Prick potatoes all over with a fork or the tip of a sharp knife. Bake the potatoes in a preheated 350-degree oven until done. Potatoes are done when they can be pricked easily with a fork.

Holding each potato with a dishcloth or potholder, scrape the insides into a mixing bowl. Add the egg yolk, cheeses, seasonings, butter, and cream and beat well until the potato mixture is completely smooth. Put in a pastry bag and pipe back into the potato skins. If you don't have a pastry bag, you can simply spoon it back in. Top with a little additional Cheddar cheese and brown the stuffed potatoes briefly under the broiler before serving. Yield: 4 servings.

Wisconsin grows all the major commercial potatoes—russet or baking potatoes, yellow boilers like Yukon Gold, and the red that consumers commonly think of as new potatoes since they come to market young and small. At area farmers' markets you can find some of the more exotic varieties like blue potatoes and fingerlings, which are delicious and fun to serve. Potatoes, natives of the Peruvian Andes, are adaptable and good cooked just about any way.

Rice is another versatile workhorse in the cook's repertoire. It's a grain, rather than a vegetable, but we include it here because it works so well with vegetables. Although the recipe given here is used at Quivey's for the Chicken Popover, it would be equally good with the recipes for stuffed chicken breasts or a number of other dishes.

Rice

$^1/_4$ cup finely diced celery
$^1/_4$ cup finely diced onion
$^1/_4$ cup finely diced mushrooms
$^1/_4$ cup finely diced bell pepper, red or green
4 tablespoons butter
1 cup rice
3 cups chicken stock
$^1/_4$ cup (2 ounces) tomato juice
1 teaspoon fresh sage
Salt and pepper to taste

. . . . .

Sauté the vegetables in the butter until the onions are translucent. Add the rice and stir to coat completely. Heat the chicken stock with the tomato juice and sage and add to the rice. Cover and simmer gently until all the liquid is absorbed and the rice is tender, about 30 minutes. Yield: 4 servings.

Chef Craig says that "the longer this cooks the better." It should be "that nice golden color you don't see anymore." Originally, the recipe came from Freddie Vol at the Bavaria Sausage Kitchen.

Quivey's Sauerkraut

$^1/_4$ pound bacon
4 pounds sauerkraut, drained
$^1/_2$ cup brown sugar
6 tablespoons white vinegar
$^1/_2$ teaspoon salt
$^1/_2$ teaspoon freshly grated black pepper
2 tablespoons Bavarian mustard

. . . . .

Cut the bacon in small pieces and brown them in a heavy-bottom kettle. Add in the sauerkraut and other ingredients, stir to mix, and simmer, covered, on very low heat. Remember, the longer this cooks, the better. It should turn a golden color and the flavor should be noticeably enhanced. This is used with many dishes at Quivey's, including braised goose. It is also served with bratwurst and kalberwurst. Yield: 4 pounds.

Americans consume about 359 million pounds of sauerkraut each year, about 1$^1/_2$ pounds per person. If all sauerkraut were made the Quivey's way, the average would be much higher.

Squash is one of the few native American foods we commonly enjoy today. Hubbard-type squash were cultivated in the Andes Mountains of Argentina and Peru 5,000 years ago, and were carried into North America by the early Spanish explorers.

Winter squash is a long-term "keeper" in the root cellar, but it's still better when used fresh like its more fragile summer counterparts. Try this dish when butternut squash first becomes available in the fall. It's wonderful all by itself or with stuffed pork chops, or it could even be a new entry in the Thanksgiving sweepstakes for most favored vegetable.

Squash Timbales

1¼ cups pureed squash
1 teaspoon peeled, grated
   fresh ginger
4 eggs
½ cup whipping cream

½ teaspoon salt
½ teaspoon white pepper
½ teaspoon allspice
2 tablespoons maple syrup
Bread crumbs

. . . . . .

Quarter one large butternut squash, clean the seeds out of the cavity, and place it, cut side down, in a glass or stainless steel baking dish. Barely cover the bottom of the dish with water and roast the squash in a hot oven (425 degrees) for 20-25 minutes or until tender. Cool and remove the meat from the rind, then puree it in a food processor or blender.

Generously grease 4 individual timbale molds. (Custard cups may be substituted.) Sprinkle with bread crumbs until the molds are completely covered. Set aside. Preheat oven to 325 degrees. Put the teakettle on to simmer.

Add the ginger to the squash and add the eggs, one at a time, beating well after each addition. Beat in the cream and spices, being sure all ingredients are incorporated evenly. Pour the squash into the timbale molds or custard cups. Put the cups in a shallow roasting pan and add simmering water to the pan to a depth of 2 inches. Bake for about 25 minutes or until a knife inserted in the center comes out clean. If not serving immediately, hold the timbales in the hot water bath until ready to unmold onto plates or serving platter. Yield: 4 large or 6 small timbales.

If you've ever been served shoestring sweet potatoes in a restaurant and wanted to try them at home, here's how. They are delicious, a wonderful garnish for many meats, and fun to eat. Kids love them.

Shoestring Sweet Potatoes

2 good-size sweet potatoes   Salt & pepper to taste
1 cup flour   Oil for frying

. . . . . .

Peel the sweet potatoes. Heat the oil to 375 degrees. Using a $1/8$-inch julienne blade on the food processor, julienne the potatoes into long strings. Season the flour with the salt and pepper. Dredge the strings in the flour. Fry until colored and crisp. Drain on absorbent paper. Excellent with steaks or rare duck breast. Yield: Shoestrings for 4 servings.

These stuffed tomatoes are easy to prepare, and make a great accompaniment to a roast. In summer, they may be enjoyed when served with a tossed salad for a light lunch.

Stuffed Tomato

4 large ripe tomatoes
$^1/_4$ cup salad croutons
$^1/_2$ cup freshly grated Parmesan
$^1/_2$ cup fresh spinach
$^1/_4$ cup olive oil
$^1/_4$ cup fresh basil
$^1/_2$ teaspoon black pepper

Preheat oven to 350 degrees. Cut off the top of each tomato. With a melon baller, core and scoop out a hollow large enough to hold the filling. Process the croutons and the cheese in the food processor. Add the rest of the ingredients, except the tomatoes, and process or chop coarsely. Top each tomato with the stuffing and press gently into the tomato. Drizzle with a little olive oil and bake about 10 minutes. Yield: 4 servings.

*Wisconsin's Native Americans are among the major produc-
ers of wild rice. This grain, a first cousin of corn, is delicious
and goes wonderfully with just about any meat. It also makes
a splendid salad in summer when mixed with fresh vegetables
such as peas and dressed with olive oil and lemon juice.*

*This particular recipe was created to go with Chicken Bond
(page 84), although you may use it successfully with a number of dishes. Wild rice is particularly good with game dishes.*

Wild Rice
for Chicken Bond

2 tablespoons olive oil
3 tablespoons white wine
1 shallot, minced
$^1/_2$ leek (white part), cleaned and finely diced
1 finely diced celery rib
$^1/_2$ finely diced red bell pepper
$^1/_2$ teaspoon coriander
$^1/_2$ tablespoon fresh sage
$^1/_2$ cup dried cherries
1 cup wild rice
3 cups chicken stock

. . . . . .

Rinse the wild rice in a colander under cold, running water.
Sauté the leek, celery, and pepper in the olive oil and wine.
Heat the stock. Add the rice and stir to coat thoroughly. Add
the spices and dried cherries. Add the simmering stock and
cover. Simmer gently until all the liquid is absorbed, about
30 minutes. Yield: 4 servings.

*"The autumn duck
season was a glad
time for the
Indians also, for
they feasted and
grew fat not only
on the ducks but
on the wild rice,
large quantities
of which they
gathered as they
glided through
the midst of the
generous crop in
canoes, bending
down handfuls
over the sides, and
beating out the
grain with small
paddles."*

—John Muir, The
Story of My
Boyhood and
Youth, *1912*

Here are some recipes for sauces that are used on more than one dish at Quivey's, sauces that are special because of their ingredients or background. Generally they are ones you can use on many different dishes and we have included chef Craig's recommendations for using each one.

There are also a few other recipes that did not fit neatly into any of the other categories, but that are served often at Quivey's and that might find a welcome place in your home menu planning, too.

Following is a marinade for chicken, one of our most popular grilled meats. Try this marinade for your next chicken cook-out, and add some fresh vegetables for the grill along with the chicken. Onions, mushrooms, red bell peppers, and chunks of zucchini would make a pretty and delicious accompaniment.

Chicken Marinade

$^1/_2$ cup fresh lemon juice
$^1/_2$ cup olive oil
$^1/_4$ cup red wine vinegar
$^1/_2$ medium onion, diced fine
1 tablespoon Dijon-style mustard
1 teaspoon oregano
1 teaspoon dry mustard
2 cloves minced garlic
1 tablespoon basil
1 teaspoon rosemary

. . . . . .

Put all the ingredients in a mixing bowl and beat well to blend thoroughly. Use as you would any marinade.

In a favorable spring with plenty of early moisture, morel mushrooms grow in profusion in the woods and abandoned orchards of southern Wisconsin. Quivey's gratefully accepts all the morels that people bring them, and they freeze what they cannot use immediately. Morels can also be dried successfully. The University of Wisconsin-Extension offers a pamphlet describing how to dry woodland mushrooms. They can easily be reconstituted in a little water or broth. Here is a wonderful sauce to use with either fresh or preserved morels. It's good with beef tenderloin, veal dishes like chops and rouladen, and with chicken breasts.

Morel Cream Sauce

$^{1}/_{2}$ cup diced morels
2 cups white mushrooms
$^{1}/_{2}$ cup diced leeks
4 cloves garlic, diced
2 tablespoons clarified butter
$^{1}/_{2}$ cup veal or chicken stock
$^{1}/_{4}$ cup coarsely chopped parsley
1 tablespoon Madeira
Salt to taste
$^{1}/_{2}$ teaspoon thyme
$1^{1}/_{3}$ cups whipping cream
1 egg yolk

. . . . . .

If the morels are frozen, chop while still frozen. Sauté the morels, mushrooms, leeks, and garlic in the butter till most of the moisture is gone. Add the stock, parsley, Madeira, salt, and thyme and reduce. Add the cream and reduce just until the sauce coats the back of a spoon. Remove from the heat and beat in the egg yolk, returning to the heat just to thicken slightly. The sauce should still be on the thin side. Hold warm. Yield: $1^{1}/_{2}$ cups sauce.

This sauce is served with pan-fried lake trout, as well as other fried fish served at Quivey's. It's good with any fried fish.

Phoenix Sauce

1 cup good mayonnaise
$^1/_2$ tablespoon capers
$^1/_2$ teaspoon dry mustard
$^1/_2$ tablespoon Dijon-style mustard
1 minced gherkin
$^1/_4$ teaspoon cayenne
1 tablespoon combined fresh chopped parsley, chives, and
    thyme
$^1/_2$ teaspoon garlic paste
1 tablespoon fresh horseradish

Put all the ingredients into a medium mixing bowl and beat well to blend thoroughly. May be refrigerated until needed. Yield: 10-12 servings.

Pork Ginger Mustard Sauce is used at Quivey's with pork tenderloin medallions, although it could be used equally well with a whole pork tenderloin or with chops from the grill.

Pork Ginger Mustard Sauce

2 tablespoons butter
1 bunch green onions, sliced fine diagonally
1 tablespoon minced garlic
1 tablespoon minced fresh ginger
2 tablespoons whipping cream
2 tablespoons cider vinegar
1 tablespoon fresh lemon juice
4 cups pork or chicken stock, reduced to 1 cup
2 tablespoons coarse-grain Dijon-style mustard
Salt to taste

. . . . . .

Sauté the scallions, garlic, and ginger in the butter until crisp and hot. Add the vinegar and reduce. Add the cream and reduce. Add the stock, bring to a boil, simmer for 3 minutes. Add the mustard and cook to the desired consistency. Yield: Enough for 1 tenderloin or 6-8 medallions.

This compote is used at Quivey's in plating steaks. Some of the compote is spooned onto a plate and the steak is placed on top. It will go well with grilled chicken or pork, also. It's a good way to use surplus red peppers from your garden.

Roasted Red Pepper & Onion Compote

5 red bell peppers
1 red onion
3 tablespoons olive oil
2 tablespoons sugar
3 tablespoons cider vinegar
1^1/$_2$ tablespoons Dijon-style mustard

. . . . . .

Roast and peel red peppers. Julienne and reserve. Slice onion thinly into rings. Put the oil and the onion rings in a saute pan, cover, and sweat the onion rings till very soft, about 20 minutes. Uncover, add sugar, and let color slightly. Add the rest of the ingredients and warm through. May be made ahead and reheated. Yield: 8 servings.

Sheboygan Sauce is so named, according to Craig, because Joe Garton and his cousin Dan, who was the restaurant's first manager, come from there. And in Sheboygan there is a certain method to grilling meat, whether it's famous Sheboygan bratwurst or steak. That method includes a sauce that is used to baste the meat, is used warm to hold the meat for serving, and is sometimes used as a marinade. It's generally made, Craig says, with "a little of this and a little of that"—in other words, whatever the Sheboygan chef finds in the kitchen cupboard. When Craig created one for a New York strip that was being cooked on a spit outdoors, it seemed only right and natural to name it Sheboygan Sauce. Craig says it's an all-purpose sauce good for any beef or pork to be grilled.

Sheboygan Sauce

$^1/_2$ cup melted butter
$^1/_3$ cup Worcestershire sauce
$^1/_2$ cup good barbecue sauce
1 teaspoon thyme
1 teaspoon seasoning salt
1 teaspoon garlic salt
1 teaspoon dry mustard
$^1/_2$ teaspoon Tabasco sauce
1 teaspoon Chinese five spice powder

. . . . . .

Put all the ingredients together in a small saucepan and simmer gently for 15 minutes. Need more? Just double everything, tasting as you go. It should be seasoned to your taste. Yield: Enough to grill 3-4 strip steaks.

Summer brings many good things to Wisconsin, one of the best being vine-ripened tomatoes. Usually there are more to-matoes than one can deal with, and Quivey's has a wonder-ful tomato coulis that will put some of them to very good use.

Coulis is a French term which, according to The Chef's Com-panion, *originally meant the strained juices from cooked meat, but has come to mean a thick sauce or puree.*

This recipe is used with the baked lake trout in horseradish crust (page 115). The tomatoes are a good counterpoint to the horseradish. The recipe is also used with the baked salmon (page 116) and with pasta dishes. It's a versatile dish and a great way to use fresh garden tomatoes.

Tomato Coulis

12 fresh, ripe tomatoes, peeled, cut up, and seeded*
$^1/_2$ tablespoon chopped fresh basil
2 cloves garlic, minced
2 shallots, diced
$^1/_2$ tablespoon chopped fresh oregano
2 tablespoons olive oil
Salt and pepper to taste

In a large pan sauté the herbs, garlic, and shallots in the olive oil. Add the tomatoes and cook just until hot through. Run tomatoes through a food processor, strain, and keep warm. Yield: 8 servings.

* The best way to peel a fresh tomato is to plunge it in boiling water and then in cold water. The skin should slip right off.

A Mother's Day Brunch at the Stone House

BUFFET TABLE

Cherry fritters

Butterhorns

Lemon-poppyseed bread

Buttermilk puffs

Gingersnaps

Cinnamon rolls

Strawberry muffins

Fruit and vegetable trays

Smoked trout salad

Cheese assortment

ENTREES

*Smoked gouda and onion quiche with ham crust, served
with American fried potatoes and asparagus*

Chicken popover with mushrooms, cream sauce, and rice

Smoked turkey popover with broccoli, cheddar sauce, and rice

Asparagus omelette with cheddar cheese and American fried potatoes

Roast sirloin with American fried potatoes

French toast with cinnamon swirl, syrup, and bacon

*Farmers omelette with ham, potatoes, and cheese, served
with sautéed apples*

*Baked trout with green onion, dill, and mustard butter,
served with parmesan potato*

DESSERTS

Apple crisp with ice cream

Turtle pie

Hot fudge sundae

Desserts

Quivey's holds to tradition in the realm of desserts just as it does in the rest of its menu. Many people think immediately of old-fashioned steamed puddings whenever they think of Quivey's Grove. Others look forward to Quivey's fresh fruit pies, which reflect the bounty of the season—strawberries in June, raspberries in August, apples and pumpkin through the fall. Dishes such as apple crisp and homemade strawberry ice cream are also seasonal treats. But some of our kitchen creations are just wicked indulgences. Kahlua Fudge Bottom and Turtle Pie are both suitable rewards for living in the late twentieth century.

> Did you ever realize how many strange names there are for some early American desserts? Apple Pan Dowdy is related to Apple Grunt and Apple Charlotte . . . Blueberry Grunt is—no one knows quite why—a grunt rather than a buckle.
>
> *From* James Beard's American Cookery

The differences between these desserts are not as marked as the similarity. A pandowdy is, according to *The Chef's Companion,* "An early American dessert, probably from New England, of sliced apples mixed with cider, brown sugar or molasses, spices and butter, covered with biscuit dough, and baked." The same book defines a grunt as "Stewed fruit topped with dumplings, an early American dessert similar to slump." It gives the same definition for slump, adding only ". . . served with cream, popular in eighteenth and nineteenth century America. Louisa May Alcott named her home in Concord, Massachusetts 'Apple Slump.'" The book does not define either crisp or buckle, which may simply be other names for almost the same dessert.

Sidney Dean's wonderful book, *Cooking American*, features recipes from three generations of devoted cooks, in addition to those of friends scattered all over the country. Here is his Apple Slump, certainly worthy of having a home named for it.

Apple Slump, Old New England

Pare, core and slice apples almost to fill a deep, well-buttered earthenware dish. Sprinkle filling with $^1/_2$ to 1 cup of sugar, depending on tartness of fruit, and $^1/_2$ teaspoon salt. Grate a little nutmeg over the mixture and add 2 tablespoons water. Cover the dish with a rich, quick biscuit crust, bake 10 minutes in hot (450 degree) oven, and reduce heat to 350 degrees until crust is a rich brown, about 45 minutes. Remove the dish from the oven, loosen the crust around the sides with a knife, and invert the contents on a platter, apple side uppermost. Dot steaming surface with butter, sift on a little more nutmeg and return platter to oven until butter melts. Serve with hard or molasses sauce.

It should be remembered that many of Wisconsin's early settlers came here from New England and upper New York State.

The foregoing slump is an American version of the French country dessert, Tart Tatin. A Tart Tatin is an apple tart that is served upside down. Legend tells us that the mademoiselles Tatin, upon taking their apple tart from the oven, dropped it on the floor. They simply slid it onto a plate and served it that way. Their guests were so taken with it that they served it that way from then on.

Mr. Dean also mentions Royal George Pudding, which turns out to be an apple pie with a rich, sour cream crust. How it got its name must be an interesting story that unfortunately isn't told. He also mentions an apple roly-poly, which is simply apples cut and sliced onto biscuit dough that's then rolled up, jelly roll fashion, and steamed like a pudding. There seem to be endless variations on the basic theme of fruit baked with sugar, spices, and some kind of butter-and-flour combination, either as biscuits, pie crust, or a crumb topping or bottom.

Quivey's serves both Apple Crisp and Peach Pan Dowdy. No slumps, buckles, or grunts, however.

Apple Crisp

APPLES
6 cups apples, peeled, cored & sliced
1 tablespoon lemon juice
2 tablespoons butter, melted
$^1/_2$ cup sugar
$^3/_4$ teaspoon cinnamon
$^1/_4$ teaspoon nutmeg
3 tablespoons cornstarch

CRISP
4 ounces ($^1/_2$ cup) butter
1 cup brown sugar
1 cup oatmeal
$^2/_3$ cup flour
$^3/_4$ teaspoon baking powder
$^3/_4$ teaspoon cinnamon
$^1/_4$ teaspoon nutmeg

. . . . . .

Preheat oven to 350 degrees. Get out a 9 x 13-inch pan.

Sprinkle the apples with the lemon juice and butter. Combine the sugar, spices, and cornstarch and toss with the apples. Put the apples in the pan.

Cut the butter into the brown sugar, oatmeal, flour, baking powder, and spices until the mixture resembles coarse meal.

Cover the pan with a piece of foil; place the pan in the oven and bake for 20 minutes. Remove the pan from the oven and remove the foil. Sprinkle the topping over the apples, return the pan to the oven, and bake another 15-18 minutes or till nicely browned. Serve with vanilla ice cream or unsweetened whipped cream. Yield: 6-8 servings.

"… to our delight, we found plenty of hazelnuts, and in a few places abundance of wild apples. They were desperately sour, and we used to fill our pockets with them and dare each other to eat one without making a face— no easy feat."

—John Muir, The Story of My Boyhood and Youth, *1912*

Butterhorns are a traditional eastern European delicacy. In the Paprika Weiss cookbook, they are called Dios szarvacskak or Walnut horns. The recipe used at Quivey's came from Joe Garton's grandmother. When they were first served at Quivey's Grove at Sunday brunch, the kitchen staff quickly found themselves overwhelmed by the demand, and by the third or fourth week were making eight hundred butterhorns each Saturday night.

These are unique in that yeast is used for its flavor, but not as a leavening agent, since the butterhorns are not given enough time to rise.

Butterhorns

1 cup flour
1 tablespoon sugar
$^1/_4$ teaspoon salt
8 tablespoons butter
1 teaspoon yeast ($^1/_2$ packet)
2 tablespoons water, 110 degrees
1 egg yolk

FILLING
1 egg white
3 tablespoons confectioners sugar
Pinch cream of tartar
$^1/_2$ cup brown sugar (approx.)

FROSTING
$1^1/_4$ cups confectioners sugar
3 tablespoons butter, softened
1 teaspoon vanilla extract
2 teaspoons milk

$^1/_4$ cup ground walnuts

. . . . . .

Mix together the flour, salt, and sugar, and cut in the butter in the food processor until the mixture resembles coarse meal. Dissolve the yeast in the warm water. Beat the egg yolk well and add it to the yeast mixture.

Make a well in the flour and pour in the yeast mixture. Mix lightly. The dough will be sticky and you might need additional flour. Divide the dough into 2 pieces. Chill for 15 minutes. Roll each piece out into a circle about $1/8$-inch thick. Cut into 12 triangles.

Preheat oven to 300 degrees. Butter and flour two cookie sheets. To make a meringue, beat the egg white till frothy. Add the cream of tartar and with mixer on high speed beat egg white, adding a spoon of sugar at a time until all the sugar is incorporated and the egg white forms stiff peaks.

Fill a pastry bag with the meringue and pipe a tablespoon of the filling onto the outside edge of the triangles. Sprinkle lightly with brown sugar and gently roll up. As you place each triangle on the baking sheet, bend it at both ends so it forms a crescent with the tip in the middle. Put the baking sheet in the oven for 12-14 minutes. Cool and frost.

For the frosting, cream the butter with the confectioners' sugar, and add in the vanilla. Add the milk to get the right consistency. Frost the cooled butterhorns and sprinkle with the ground walnuts. Yield: about 24 butterhorns.

There are probably as many carrot cake recipes as there are people who make it regularly. Here's Quivey's version, which is so popular that it has been made up as a wedding cake.

Carrot Cake

CAKE
3 eggs
2 cups brown sugar
1 1/2 cups canola oil
2 teaspoons vanilla extract
2 cups flour
1 teaspoon baking soda
1/4 teaspoon each of salt, allspice, nutmeg, ginger
1 teaspoon cinnamon

1 1/4 cups crushed pineapple, drained
1 cup finely chopped walnuts
8 ounces (1 cup) grated carrots

ICING
6 ounces cream cheese
4 ounces butter, softened
1/2 teaspoon vanilla extract
1 cup powdered sugar

Preheat oven to 350 degrees. Grease and flour two 8-inch round cake pans.

Beat the eggs with the brown sugar and oil, add the vanilla, mixing well. Sift together flour, baking soda, salt, and spices. Combine the pineapple, walnuts, and carrots. Add carrot mixture to egg mixture. Add the sifted dry ingredients, folding in gently, just until all are well moistened. If using an electric mixer, use low speed. Turn the batter into the prepared pans and put them into the oven.

Bake for 25 minutes. The cake is done if it springs back when pressed in the center. Cool for a few minutes, then turn out on a cake rack and cool completely before icing.

To make the icing, cream together butter and cream cheese, add sugar and vanilla, and beat until perfectly smooth. Spread icing on the bottom cake layer, then put the second layer on top and cover it with icing. Yield: one 8-inch layer cake.

This is one of Quivey's most popular chocolate desserts, a true indulgence for the confirmed chocoholic. It is a flourless cake, similar to the nut-based cakes so popular in Eastern Europe.

Chocolate Nut Torte

TORTE
2 tablespoons strong coffee
6 ounces semi-sweet
    chocolate
$^1/_2$ cup butter
3 eggs
1 cup sugar
1 teaspoon vanilla extract
$^1/_2$ teaspoon salt
$^1/_2$ cup flour
$^1/_4$ cup finely-ground nuts

GLAZE
3 tablespoons light corn
    syrup
1 tablespoon water
1 tablespoon butter
$^1/_8$ teaspoon cinnamon
2 ounces semi-sweet
    chocolate
$^1/_4$ cup coarsely chopped
    nuts

. . . . .

Preheat oven to 350 degrees. Grease and dust with cocoa an 8- or 9-inch cake pan.

Over hot water, melt the chocolate and butter with the coffee and allow it to cool. Beat the eggs with the sugar, vanilla, and salt on high speed for 10 minutes. Blend in the chocolate mixture. Mix the ground nuts and flour together and fold that into the batter, mixing thoroughly. Spread it into the prepared pan and place it into the oven.

Bake for 30 minutes for a 9-inch pan; 45 minutes for an 8-inch pan. Remove from oven and cool 10 minutes. Remove cake from pan onto a cake rack and cool completely.

Bring the corn syrup and butter to a boil, then remove from heat and add the water, cinnamon, and chocolate. Spread on the cooled torte and garnish with the coarsely chopped nuts. Yield: one 8- or 9-inch torte.

This dessert is so popular, it's served year 'round at Quivey's. At cranberry harvest time, simply purchase a couple of extra bags of the berries and toss them in the freezer.

Cranberry Steamed Pudding

Wisconsin is the number two cranberry-producing state in the nation, harvesting nearly 1.5 million barrels annually from the bogs in the central sand counties.

1^2/$_3$ cups flour
2 teaspoons baking powder
^{1}/$_4$ teaspoon salt
^{1}/$_4$ teaspoon allspice
^{1}/$_2$ cup chopped fresh cranberries
^{1}/$_2$ cup chopped pecans
^{1}/$_4$ cup milk
Grated rind & juice of 1 orange
^{1}/$_4$ cup butter, softened
^{3}/$_4$ cup sugar
2 eggs

. . . . . .

Preheat oven to 350 degrees. Generously grease 10 4-ounce custard cups. Put teakettle on to simmer.

In a medium mixing bowl, sift together flour, baking powder, salt, and allspice. Set aside. Chop the cranberries and pecans. Grate the rind of the orange. Squeeze ^{1}/$_4$ cup of orange juice and set aside. In a mixing bowl cream the butter and sugar until fluffy. Add the eggs one at a time, beating well after each addition. Alternately add the flour mixture and the milk and orange juice to the sugar mixture and stir until smooth. Add the cranberries and pecans. Fill the custard cups two-thirds full. Cover cups with lightly greased foil and put into a deep roasting pan. Pour simmering water in pan to depth of 2 inches. Cover pan with foil and put into oven. Bake 25-30 minutes. If done, puddings should spring back when pressed in center. Serve with brandy cream sauce (page 159) or a hard sauce. Yield: 10 servings.

This dessert is a signature dish of Quivey's Grove, well-known to long-time patrons and reason enough for many people to come often to Quivey's for dinner. The prized recipe comes from chef Craig Kuenning's grandmother.

Chocolate Steamed Pudding
with Ellie's Mom's Sauce

PUDDING
1 tablespoon butter
1^1/$_2$ ounces unsweetened chocolate
1 egg
^{3}/$_4$ cup sugar
^{1}/$_2$ teaspoon vanilla extract
1 cup coffee, cooled
1^1/$_2$ cups flour, sifted
^{1}/$_4$ teaspoon salt
1^1/$_2$ teaspoons baking powder

SAUCE
2^1/$_2$ cups confectioners' sugar
2 eggs
6 tablespoons butter
^{1}/$_4$ teaspoon salt
1^1/$_2$ teaspoons vanilla extract
1 cup whipping cream

. . . . . .

Preheat oven to 350 degrees. Butter 8 (6-ounce) custard cups. Chill a large mixing bowl and beaters or wire whisk in freezer. Put teakettle on to simmer.

In top of a double boiler, over low heat, melt butter and chocolate. Set aside to cool. Beat the egg and sugar together, add vanilla, beat again. Add the chocolate and beat once more. Add cooled coffee and blend well. Sift dry ingredients together and add to chocolate mixture. The batter should be perfectly smooth. Fill cups with chocolate mixture. Cover each cup tightly with a piece of foil that has been lightly greased.

Set cups in a baking pan. Add $1/2$-inch hot water to baking pan, cover the pan with foil and place into the oven. Steam for 30 minutes. Cool slightly before unmolding. Serve warm with Ellie's Mom's Sauce.

For the sauce, combine the first five ingredients in a bowl, mixing until creamy and smooth. Pour the whipping cream into the chilled bowl and beat with the chilled whisk or beaters until slightly thickened. Begin to fold in the egg mixture, maintaining as much air as possible in the whipped cream. Whip by hand until smooth. Yield: 8 individual puddings and 3 cups sauce.

In his American Cookery, *James Beard says, "Fool is a fruit dish that the English brought with them and which has spread through the country. The south adopted it first, followed by New England and Pennsylvania. It is still a great delicacy and can be made with rhubarb, raspberries, strawberries, greengage plum, as well as with gooseberries."*

Quivey's recipe calls for any fresh fruit.

Fresh Fruit Fool

1 cup pureed, fresh fruit
2 tablespoons fruit-flavored liqueur such as kirsch
   or framboise
$^1/_2$ tablespoon gelatin
$^1/_3$ cup sugar
1 cup whipping cream
1 tablespoon corn syrup
Mint sprigs

· · · · · ·

Puree the selected fruit to make one cup. Dissolve the gelatin in the liqueur. Put the fruit and sugar in a heavy-bottom saucepan. Stir to blend and dissolve sugar. Add the gelatin mixture and bring just to a boil. Remove from the heat, stir to blend, and allow to cool slightly. Refrigerate until firm.

Whip the cream with corn syrup until stiff peaks form. Be careful not to overbeat.

Whip the gelatin mixture until soft and light. Fold some of the whipped cream into the gelatin mixture to lighten. Then fold the gelatin mixture into the cream and spoon into tall, stemmed glasses. Chill to set. Garnish with a slice of fruit and a mint sprig. Yield: 4 servings.

Ginger was a very popular spice in early American house-holds—witness gingerbread, ginger snaps, ginger cookies, molasses cookies, cakes; spice cake, and applesauce cake. In the 1870s this couplet was popular in autograph albums:

> *"And may your happiness ever spread*
> *Like butter on hot gingerbread."*

Gingerbread even became an invaluable aid in the Revolutionary War. In 1776 the British were camped for the winter just outside Trenton, New Jersey, a bit north of Philadelphia. In Philadelphia a German baker who had settled there went to General Washington at Valley Forge. He proposed that he take gingerbread to the British encampment and get permission to sell it to the Hessian soldiers.

The Hessian soldiers had been sold into the British army by their prince and were far from home. The baker sold them gingerbread and, as he did, he told them of the opportunities available to them in this marvelous new country, that they could have freedom and land just for living on it. The desertion rate among the Hessians rose sharply. The baker and his gingerbread had done their work well.

We are indebted to Mr. Sidney Dean for the following bit of lore on the subject of puddings, steamed ones in particular.

"Generous home helpings leave the blessed who receive them feeling as pleasantly replete as Charles Lamb [the well-known Victorian writer] in the stage coach at Kentish Town. When a would-be passenger asked the coachman, 'Are you quite full inside?' the incorrigible Charles put his head through the window and said: 'I am quite full inside, that last piece of pudding did the business for me.'"

Steamed Gingerbread Pudding
With Brandy Cream Sauce

PUDDING
1/2 cup sugar
1 egg
1/2 cup butter, melted
1/2 cup molasses
1/2 cup honey
1 cup hot water
2 1/2 cups all-purpose flour
1 1/2 teaspoon baking soda
1 teaspoon cinnamon

1 1/2 teaspoon ginger
1/2 teaspoon salt

SAUCE
1 cup whipping cream
1 egg yolk
1/3 cup sifted confectioners'
   sugar
1 1/2 tablespoons brandy

Steamed puddings are best served warm. Unlike more delicate cakes, they can be made ahead and rewarmed in a microwave oven without loss of quality.

Lightly grease eight custard cups and put them into a large open roasting pan. Preheat oven to 350 degrees. Put the teakettle on to simmer.

Beat the sugar and eggs till fluffy. Add the butter and mix well. Sift the dry ingredients together. Combine molasses, honey, and hot water. Alternately add wet and dry mixtures to the egg mixture, stirring just to combine. When all ingredients have been blended together, fill custard cups two-thirds full. Cover the cups tightly with lightly greased foil.

Pour simmering water around cups, halfway up sides of cups. Bake for 45 minutes to an hour or until the pudding springs back at a touch. Check periodically to make sure water does not boil away. Add hot water if necessary.

For the sauce, beat cream with a mixer at high speed until it forms soft peaks. Hold. In another bowl, whisk together egg yolk, sugar, and brandy. Combine the egg mixture with the cream mixture and pour into a covered container. Refrigerate until ready to serve.

Serve the pudding warm, topped with Brandy Cream Sauce. Yield: 6 servings.

Gingerbread

To make your
gingerbread a little
more elegant and
flavorful, sprinkle
the top with
chopped candied
ginger just before
putting it into the
oven.

6 tablespoons margarine
6 tablespoons sugar
1 egg
$^1/_4$ cup molasses
$^1/_4$ cup honey
$^1/_2$ cup + 2 tablespoons hot water
3 tablespoons white rum
2 cups flour
$1^1/_2$ teaspoons baking soda
$^1/_2$ teaspoon cinnamon
$1^1/_4$ teaspoons ginger
$^1/_2$ teaspoon ground cloves

. . . . . .

Grease and flour one 9-inch square or round pan. Preheat
the oven to 350 degrees.

Cream the margarine and sugar together, then add the egg.
Mix together the molasses, honey, water, and rum. Beat in
the molasses mixture. Mix the dry ingredients together in a
bowl. Add into the liquid mixture, stirring to blend well.
Pour into prepared pan and put in the oven.

Bake, checking after 35 minutes. Cake is done when a tooth-
pick inserted in the center of the cake comes out dry. Yield:
6-8 servings.

Gingersnaps have been a favorite fall cookie for generations because they go so well with cider and crisp apples. Ginger cookies are also integral to any Christmas celebration. One of our testers for this recipe was five-year-old Lars Koch, whose mom, Anne Behrmann, was one of the home cooks. A cookie recipe is not tested until it's kid-tested.

Gingersnaps

2 cups flour
³/₄ teaspoon baking soda
1¹/₂ teaspoons ginger
³/₄ teaspoon cinnamon
¹/₄ teaspoon cloves
¹/₄ cup butter, softened
1 cup sugar
1 egg
¹/₄ cup molasses
1¹/₂ tablespoons vinegar

. . . . . .

Sift together the flour, baking soda, and spices. Cream the butter with the sugar until light and fluffy. Add in the egg and beat well. Add in the molasses and vinegar and mix well. Then add in the flour mix until all ingredients are incorporated. Refrigerate the dough until firm, then roll into one-inch logs. When rolling into logs, coat your hands with flour to make dough easier to handle. Freeze until firm.

Preheat the oven to 375 degrees. Grease 2 cookie sheets.

Cut ¹/₄-inch pieces from the logs, place onto the greased cookie sheets, and sprinkle with white granulated sugar. Bake for 8-10 minutes, remove from pans, and cool on wire racks. Store in airtight containers. Yield: 6-7 dozen cookies.

Quivey's also uses these cookies when making Sauerbraten.

What makes these steamed puddings "Irish" is the use of Irish whiskey in the batter. A perfect dessert for St. Patrick's Day.

Irish Steamed Puddings

^{1}/$_3$ cup butter, softened
^{2}/$_3$ cup brown sugar
1 egg
^{1}/$_4$ teaspoon allspice
1 teaspoon cinnamon
1^1/$_2$ cups flour
1 teaspoon baking powder
^{1}/$_4$ cup Irish whiskey
1 cup milk
1 cup apples, peeled, chopped fine
^{1}/$_2$ cup raisins

. . . . . .

In the 1820s and 1830s, many Irishmen came to Wisconsin to work in the lead mines in and around Mineral Point. The Irish potato famine of the 1840s prompted further emigration, and by 1850 more than 21,000 Irish called Wisconsin home.

Preheat the oven to 325 degrees. Grease 8 custard cups and place them into a large open roasting pan. Put the teakettle on to simmer.

In a mixing bowl, cream the butter and sugar until the mixture is combined and is fairly light in texture. Add the egg, again beating well. Sift together the spices, flour, and baking powder. Add the milk to the Irish whiskey and stir. Add the flour mixture alternately with the milk and whiskey to the butter mixture until all the ingredients are incorporated. Fold in the apples and raisins and spoon the batter into the custard cups, filling them two-thirds full.

Cover the cups with lightly greased aluminum foil. Pour simmering water to a depth of about one inch. Cover the pan with a piece of foil. Place into the oven and bake for 45 minutes to an hour or until the puddings spring back when pressed in the center. Remove and serve right away. May be served with Ellie's Mom's Sauce (page 155) or a hard sauce, garnished with a sprig of fresh mint. Yield: 8 servings.

In days past, residents of the Madison area would make pies ahead of time in the winter and simply store them in an unheated attic or shed where they froze solid. When a pie was needed for dinner, someone went out and got a frozen one and put it in the oven. That's not quite the way they do it at Quivey's, although pie is one of the mainstays of the dessert menu. Here's Quivey's pie crust.

Pie Crust

2 sticks butter ($^1/_2$ pound), cut in chunks
$2^1/_2$ cups flour
Pinch of salt
Pinch of sugar
6 tablespoons cold water

. . . . . .

Put the salt and sugar in the flour. Cut the butter into the flour, using a pastry blender. This can also be done in the food processor. Gradually add in the water, stopping when the dough begins to stick together. This should be done quickly. Don't overwater the dough.

Cut dough in half and roll out each half on a well-floured board or piece of marble. Be sure to flour the rolling pin as well before you begin to roll out the pie dough. Once rolled out to a circle larger than the pie tin, fold the dough over and lift it carefully into the pie tin.

Use the second half of the dough for the top crust. If the recipe does not call for a top crust, the dough may be wrapped in plastic, placed in a freezer bag, and frozen for later use.

Yield: one double-crust 9-inch pie, or 2 single-crust 9-inch pies.

Kahlua Fudge Bottom Pie

FILLING
2¹/₂ cups milk
1¹/₂ teaspoons gelatin
Pinch of salt
3 egg yolks, lightly beaten
³/₄ cup sugar
2¹/₂ tablespoons flour
5 ounces chocolate chips
¹/₄ cup Kahlua

1 baked 9-inch pie shell,
   cooled

TOPPING
¹/₄ teaspoon gelatin
¹/₄ cup Kahlua
1¹/₄ cups whipping cream
¹/₄ cup sifted confectioners'
   sugar

BUTTERFLY

*You're quite a
   decent looking
   girl.
You think you're in
   the social whirl,
But when of
   beauty bereft,
You've nothing else
   and you'll get
   left.*

While preparing the custard filling, put the chocolate chips and the Kahlua into a small bowl over hot water.

Put a double boiler on low heat so that the water is just simmering. Put the milk into the top of the double boiler, add the gelatin, and stir to dissolve. Add the pinch of salt, beating well to incorporate. Add the sugar and flour and stir gently until it begins to form a custard. The mixture should coat the back of a spoon dipped into it.

Stir the chocolate and Kahlua to be sure the chocolate is melted and to blend the two. Measure out about half the custard mixture and add all the Kahlua chocolate mixture to it, stirring to blend well. Gently pour this into the bottom of the baked pie shell and chill.

When the custard in the pie shell appears well set, pour the remaining custard over the Kahlua custard and chill the pie for 24 hours.

To make the topping, warm the gelatin and Kahlua together, stirring to dissolve the gelatin. Whip the cream until it begins to form stiff peaks, then add the sifted sugar and whip again. Add the Kahlua mixture to the cream, incorporating gently, and spread over the pie. Top with shaved chocolate and serve. Yield: one 9-inch pie.

This was one of the recipes cut down and tested for the book by the baking students at Madison Area Technical College. It was returned with the notation "Excellent!" at the top. See if you don't agree.

It's also one of the ingredients for Mrs. T.'s Chocolate Dessert (page 169), but these ladyfingers may be used in many other desserts, or may simply be included on a plate with other cookies and little cakes to serve with ice cream or with tea in the late afternoon.

Ladyfingers

6 eggs, separated, room temperature
1 cup sifted confectioner's sugar
1 cup sifted cake flour
$^1/_8$ teaspoon salt
1 teaspoon vanilla extract

. . . . .

Preheat the oven to 350 degrees. Cover two cookie sheets with brown paper or baking parchment. Put the O tip in a pastry bag.

Beat the egg whites, and begin to add sugar when whites begin to stiffen a little. Beat till stiff but not dry.

Beat the egg yolks until thick and lemony, then carefully fold them into the egg whites. Add the vanilla. Fold in the flour and salt. Put the batter into the pastry bag. Pipe the batter onto the paper-covered cookie sheets, making fingers about 1 x 4 inches. Lightly sift confectioner's sugar over them and put them into the oven. Bake for 12 minutes.

Remove from the oven and immediately loosen from the paper. Yield: 24 ladyfingers, 1 x 4 inches each.

Ladyfingers have been a popular confection in Wisconsin since early settlement days. The English poet John Keats mentioned "ladies' fingers" in his 1820 poem, "The Cap and Bells."

Peach Pan Dowdy

PEACHES
$^2/_3$ cup sugar
$^1/_2$ teaspoon cinnamon
$^1/_8$ teaspoon nutmeg
$^1/_8$ teaspoon allspice
5 tablespoons cornstarch
1 tablespoon lemon juice
2 tablespoon butter, melted
6 cups sliced and peeled fresh peaches

TOPPING
4 ounces ($^1/_2$ cup) butter, melted
1 cup brown sugar
1 cup oatmeal
$^3/_4$ cup flour
$^3/_4$ teaspoon baking powder
$^3/_4$ teaspoon cinnamon
$^1/_4$ teaspoon nutmeg

. . . . . .

Preheat oven to 350 degrees. Get out a 9 x 13-inch pan.

Combine the sugar with the spices and cornstarch. Sprinkle the lemon juice and melted butter over the peaches. Place the peaches in the pan, cover with aluminum foil, and put in the oven.

Cut the butter into the sugar, oatmeal, flour, baking powder, and spices until the mixture resembles coarse meal.

Bake the peaches for 15 minutes. Remove the pan from the oven and take off the foil. Sprinkle the topping over the peaches and return the pan to the oven for another 15 minutes. Serve warm with unsweetened whipped cream or vanilla, ginger, or peach ice cream. Yield: one pan, approximately 6-8 servings.

Raspberry Chiffon Pie

1 baked pie crust, cooled
$^2/_3$ cup sugar
1 tablespoon gelatin
1 cup fresh raspberries
3 egg whites, room temperature
1 teaspoon cream of tartar
$^1/_4$ cup confectioner's sugar
$^1/_2$ cup whipping cream

. . . . . .

To bake the pie crust, place a piece of aluminum foil inside the pie crust and weight it down with dried beans. Bake at 425 degrees until the pie crust is a light golden color, about 15 minutes. Cool.

Put the sugar, gelatin, and raspberries into a heavy-bottom saucepan and bring to a full, rolling boil, stirring constantly. Remove from heat and allow to cool.

Beat the egg whites until they form soft peaks. Add the cream of tartar and sugar and continue beating until stiff peaks form. Gently fold into the berry mixture.

Whip the cream until it forms stiff peaks and gently fold that into the berry and egg white mixture. Pour into the baked shell and chill. When set, this may be served with fresh whipped cream garnished with fresh raspberries and a sprig of mint. Yield: one 9-inch pie.

"An immigrant living in Beloit, Wisconsin, wrote on November 29, 1851, to friends back in Norway: 'Strawberries, raspberries, and blackberries thrive here. From these they make a wonderful dish combined with sugar and syrup, which is called pai. I can tell you it is something that glides down your throat.'"

—From the American Heritage Cookbook

When raspberries are in season, Quivey's buys all they can from local pickers. They freeze what can't immediately be used.

Another traditional use of berries besides "pai" is shortcake. A shortcake is just a sweetened biscuit that's used with fresh, slightly mashed fruit and good, rich cream or unsweetened whipped cream. Here's Quivey's shortcake recipe which you may use in season with strawberries, blueberries, or raspberries. Or even Michigan peaches.

Shortcake

1 cup flour
1¹/₂ teaspoons baking powder
1¹/₂ teaspoons sugar
¹/₄ teaspoon salt
1 tablespoon butter, cold, cut up
¹/₄ to ¹/₃ cup milk

. . . . . .

Preheat oven to 400 degrees. Get out an 8- or 9-inch round cake pan.

Using a food processor, blend the first 5 ingredients together until the mixture is mealy. Add the milk with the processor running and just barely mix. Remove the dough from the bowl, and put it into the pan. Pat out the dough evenly, cut into six or eight pielike wedges, and put the pan into the oven. Bake for 12 minutes or until biscuits are light golden-brown. Remove from oven and cool on wire rack. Yield: 6-8 shortcake biscuits.

Mrs. T. is the same grandmother whose Chocolate Steamed Pudding is featured earlier in this chapter. She seems to have been an early chocoholic. This dessert is an old one and was also known as "Picket Fence Pudding."

Mrs. T's Chocolate Dessert
or Picket Fence Pudding

Ladyfingers (page 167)
3 bars German sweet chocolate
3 tablespoons sugar
6 eggs, separated
3 tablespoon cold water
$^1/_2$ teaspoon vanilla extract

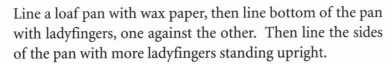

Line a loaf pan with wax paper, then line bottom of the pan with ladyfingers, one against the other. Then line the sides of the pan with more ladyfingers standing upright.

In the top of a double boiler, over hot (but not boiling) water, melt the chocolate with the sugar. Remove the chocolate mixture from the heat and beat in, one a time, the six egg yolks, beating well after each addition. Add the cold water and the vanilla extract.

In a separate bowl, beat the six egg whites until stiff peaks form. Then gently incorporate the beaten egg whites into the chocolate mixture. Pour the mixture into the loaf pan with the ladyfingers. Chill. Slice and serve as you would a meatloaf. Yield: one loaf, serving 6-8.

This dessert may well be Quivey's Grove's most famous. Certainly the recipe is the most often requested of all the desserts.

Turtle Pie

1 baked 9-inch pie shell, cooled	1 1/2 tablespoons cornstarch
1/4 cup whipping cream	3/4 teaspoon gelatin
3/4 cup brown sugar	1/4 cup milk
2 tablespoons melted butter	2 egg yolks, beaten
6 tablespoons dark corn syrup	3/4 cup chocolate chips, melted
1 cup chopped pecans	1 cup whipping cream
1 1/2 tablespoons sugar	Melted chocolate
	Pecans

. . . . . .

You will need a candy thermometer for this recipe. Put the first four ingredients into a heavy-bottom pan and bring to a simmer. Cook until the mixture reaches 227 degrees on the candy thermometer. Then add the pecans, stir well, and pour into the pie shell. Cool.

In a saucepan, blend together the sugar, cornstarch, gelatin, and milk. Heat slowly, stirring constantly, until the mixture reaches 160 degrees. Add the egg yolks and mix till smooth. Remove from heat and add the melted chocolate. Cool. While this mixture cools, whip the cream, then fold it gently into the chocolate mixture. Pour over the candy layer in the pie shell. Chill. To serve, drizzle with melted chocolate and pecans. Yield: one 9-inch pie.

BIBLIOGRAPHY

Included in this bibliography are books that you might enjoy reading for a sense of how the customs that surround what we eat have come to be. There are also some sources listed that are unavailable unless you go to the Wade House or Villa Louis and experience one of their Victorian meals.

The American Heritage Cookbook and Illustrated History of Eating and Drinking in America by the editors of *American Heritage,* published by American Heritage Publishing Company, New York, distributed by Simon & Schuster, 1964.

The Chef's Companion: A Concise Dictionary of Culinary Terms by Elizabeth Riely, published by Van Nostrand Reinhold, 1986.

Cooking American, by Sidney Dean, published by Hill & Wang, New York, 1957 (out of print).

Dictionary of Cuisine by Alexandre Dumas, translated by Louis Colman from *Le Grand Dictionnaire de Cuisine,* Avon Books, 1958 (out of print).

The Flavor of Wisconsin: An Informal History of Food and Eating in the Badger State by Harva Hachten, published by the State Historical Society of Wisconsin, Madison, Wisconsin, 1981.

A New System of Domestic Cookery by Mrs. Rundell, published by Carey & Hart, 1844 (out of print).

These are the books used in writing this cookbook. There are many more on the subject of American food and cooking. The cookbook section of any good bookstore or library is usually a good resource, as are bookstores dealing in used books—which often hide undiscovered gems on their shelves. Good hunting and bon appetit!

INDEX